FOOD TALKS

FOOD TALKS

I Loved Them, They Left Me,
But I Got Their Mothers' Recipes

RECIPE *for* LOVE

STOP WASTING TIME
WITH MR. WRONG
SO YOU CAN FIND
MR. RIGHT

DENISE TOMASETTI

NEW YORK

FOOD TALKS

I Loved Them, They Left Me, But I Got Their Mothers' Recipes
Recipe for Love
Stop wasting time with Mr. Wrong so you can find Mr. Right

Disclaimer: The Publisher and the Author make no representations or warranties with respect to the accuracy or completeness of the contents of this work and specifically disclaim all warranties, including without limitation warranties of fitness for a particular purpose. No warranty may be created or extended by sales or promotional materials. The advice and strategies contained herein may not be suitable for every situation. This work is sold with the understanding that the Publisher is not engaged in rendering legal, accounting, or other professional services. If professional assistance is required, the services of a competent professional person should be sought. Neither the Publisher nor the Author shall be liable for damages arising herefrom. The fact that an organization or website is referred to in this work as a citation and/or a potential source of further information does not mean that the Author or the Publisher endorses the information the organization or website may provide or recommendations it may make. Further, readers should be aware that internet websites listed in this work may have changed or disappeared between when this work was written and when it is read.

ISBN 978-1-61448-661-9 paperback
ISBN 978-1-61448-662-6 eBook
Library of Congress Control Number: 2013934431

Morgan James Publishing
The Entrepreneurial Publisher
5 Penn Plaza, 23rd Floor,
New York City, New York 10001
(212) 655-5470 office • (516) 908-4496 fax
www.MorganJamesPublishing.com

Editor:
Kellie Dopico

Photographer:
Rod Goodman

Cover Design by:
Rachel Lopez
www.r2cdesign.com

Interior Design by:
Bonnie Bushman
bonnie@caboodlegraphics.com

In an effort to support local communities, raise awareness and funds, Morgan James Publishing donates a percentage of all book sales for the life of each book to Habitat for Humanity Peninsula and Greater Williamsburg.

Get involved today, visit
www.MorganJamesBuilds.com.

Habitat for Humanity®
Peninsula and
Greater Williamsburg
Building Partner

Dedication

To my Mother, Grace Tomasetti
For all her love, support, and most of all,
nurturing me through food!

Contents

A Special Thank You

My sister, Yvette Tomasetti, my father, Richard Tomasetti and wife Andrea Tomasetti.

My girl friends, (AKA) "Stells": Annie Marino, Jennifer Sitomer, Caroline Bournos Diaco, Paige Loonan, Kim Baccari, Staci Rosen-Maller, Anna Carusos, Anne Dopico, Manuela Metri, Denice Rice, Dimitra Tziova, Debbie Ganz, Heather Sherin, Helen Logas, Felicity Rego Georgalas, Kimberly Rosenhaus, Agnuszka Wiesyks, Zoe Wiepert, Louise Levine, Lisa Ganz, Dina DeMartini.

Chapter One

No Introduction Needed Food Talks!

"We need to talk."

Most of us are familiar with those four dreaded little words that signal—it's over!

Wouldn't it be great to know on your first dining date if you wanted to have a second? Wouldn't it be great to stop wasting time with the wrong man? Something as simple as <u>food</u> can bring out some unknown details of your date which teaches you vital information about that person. Everything you hear, see and experience from food—all has meaning. More importantly, you get to see if you *don't* like what you've just learned about that person. From the moment a man asks you out on your first cocktail, coffee or dinner date, all you need to do—is listen. What am I listening for? How do I

1

listen? You ask? You'll know exactly what and how your food experiences speak volumes by the end of my story.

We all can relate to each other's relationships. We've all gone through "The Relationship Break-Up." We laugh, we cry at the end of each closing chapter. Every relationship is different, but most begin the same. Boy meets girl, boy asks girl out, girl says yes. Magic! You're enjoying the crazy attraction that's instinctual and best of all, when you're having sex you're not by yourself!

It could be a short courtship or a long one. Then, one day, everything changes. Surprise! Bye-bye. Are you kidding me? We've been together for years; I've met his mother and shared meals with her. Doesn't that mean anything?

Yes it does!

I gave all my love, all my time and what did I get? Well, I'll tell you what I got. I got their mothers' recipes!

Having my ex-boyfriends mothers' recipes turned out to be the icing on the cake. Their mothers' food and our shared family meals together did whisper some unknown truths to me about their sons. Once I realized that I did learn a great deal about my ex-boyfriends from their mothers' meals; the memories of other food experiences I shared with my past loves showed me that **not** just their mothers' meals spoke volumes, but all my past food experiences with them did.

I had a life changing revelation.

Food Talks!

From the venues of food and what you learn from each food experience will let you know who is really sitting across the table from you. Food is essential in our lives from survival to socializing. Food is instrumental in our relationships and our food experiences from childhood to adulthood speak truths of who we are and the people surrounding us.

Whether you're having coffee, cocktails or a meal in a restaurant, bar, lounge, at a family or friend's home and even in your own kitchen with your date—Food Talks!

All along, I did have the tools to tell me whether my relationship was right or wrong for me—especially if he was **not** right for me, long before I'd invested my heart, soul and years of my life. I simply had to listen to what food was saying!

Though you don't know me, I'm just like every woman who wants to have a healthy and happy relationship. I've learned that food and dating is a revealing combination and I would like to share these invaluable lessons with you. Maybe my realizations can change your relationship experiences for the better.

After 20 years of dating, I've learned a great deal about relationships and as you read my story, whether it's a home-cooked meal or a reservation, you too will know how food will **teach** you more about your date(s) and relationship(s) than you ever thought possible.

I've dated many different types of men, from the artist to the businessman, to the poor to the wealthy. Every man, every meal, every food experience led me to my next dating adventure and next relationship. In the middle of it all, I met their mothers. I sat at their food laden tables where my lessons began. At the time I did not realize that my food experiences with their mothers were my Dating 101 classes!

As I share with you the stories of my relationships or as I like to call them, "Main Entrées" I will refer to my ex-boyfriends by their nicknames. I'm also including a few of the men I've casually dated or as I like to call them, "Side Dishes." These Side Dish dates is where my food experiences showed me, taught me, not to waste any more time dating them.

In each chapter you'll get a flavor for what I went through to gain these precious truths by listening to the clues food has to offer. By learning from *my* mistakes you'll be able to avoid much heartache and gain the confidence to lose the losers, keep the keepers and find your date's *ingredients*—what they're made out of—what's "Tasty" and "Not Tasty" to your palate.

From my love life: relationships to casual dates and the truths conveyed to me by food experiences, you will be shown how you too can make your own "Recipe for Love."

Your "Recipe for Love" is all about what you want and don't want in a person. Whether you want a short-term or long-term relationship, a family man, a casual companion or a soul- mate, the choice is yours. I'm going to show you how to create your "Top Ten Ingredient's Card" to help find who's best for you!

Food is a great tool in your arsenal to help you stop wasting time with Mr. Wrong so you can find Mr. Right.

P.S. I'm divulging my "Main Entrées" ex-boyfriends mothers' recipes for all to have, which will give you a better taste of these men. When it comes to my "Side Dishes", I'm including my own personal side dish recipes.

When you're having a girl's night and the ladies are dishing about their relationships, these are great recipes to make!

Chapter Two

My Love Affair with Food

"**D**enise... *dinner!*"

I can still hear my mother's voice. Seven nights a week, 7:30 p.m. it was time to chow.

There were no TV dinners at my house growing up. I come from an Italian-Syrian-American background and everyone in my family loves to eat. We're so passionate about our family's recipes that we consider them actual members of the family. Each mother, aunt and uncle in my family is recognized for his or her signature dishes. At family gatherings, my mother Grace must make her meatballs and chicken cutlets, Aunt Nora makes eggplant parmesan, Aunt Maryann makes stuffed artichokes and Aunt Lori makes her roast beef. We leave the dessert to Uncle Mitchell. Most important, my Aunt Eva makes my grandmother Tata's Mediterranean dishes.

My family's recipes have always been made with love. I *felt*—and tasted—that love throughout my childhood. I saw the joy my relatives had when they cooked for each other and it thrilled me to see how food made someone smile—just by cooking a meal.

The first person I ever cooked for was my father, Richard. When I was 13 years old, after my parents' divorced, my sister, Yvette and I went on vacation with our father. I begged him to let me make dinner that evening, promising that I wouldn't burn down the rented vacation house. Although I had never cooked a meal on my own before, I had learned a great deal from watching my mother in her kitchen.

I kicked my father out of the house and told him dinner would be served at 7:30 p.m. sharp. I set the table, cooked and called out, "dinner!" I had made a fresh tomato and baby zucchini sauce over pasta and a mozzarella and basil salad. "Please, let this meal taste good," I prayed. I watched my father as he took his first bite—his eyes lit up! From that day on, my father confirmed what I always knew growing up: food was an expression of love.

Growing up, you couldn't get me out of my mother's kitchen—until I went away to boarding high school in Long Island, where an apron was not part of my uniform. Somehow the rules of boarding school and I didn't see eye to eye and getting into trouble became a subject I became an A student in. My Headmaster would punish me by making me wait on my classmates' tables, which put me back into a kitchen. Perfect! Let's just say, I had weekly visits to the Dean's office.

Off to college in New Hampshire I went and cooking became a part of my everyday life, even part of my college credits. When I left my dorm room and went out on my own, I finally got into my own kitchen and haven't left yet.

Throughout my young adulthood I fell in love and got into relationships with different men, each wonderful in his own way, but none of whom were really a match for me. As I look back now, I can see that each relationship experience helped me reach a new level of maturity. But they all came at a cost. I invested my heart, my energy and years of my life into relationships that were doomed.

The more I learned to trust my instincts, the more I came to realize I simply had to tap into the lessons gained from my own family's food experiences. I've learned to trust the messages food has to deliver and you can too. One coffee, cocktail or dinner date is all you need to make a decision over the fate of that relationship. Once you know how "food talks" to you, you'll know if you're having that second date. But when the food tells you to cut and run, go home, open a carton of ice cream and know you didn't waste any calories on him. Next!

Chapter Three

Tasty — Not Tasty

Tasty? Not Tasty?

I overheard a man speaking with his date as they were dining. Yes, I was eve's dropping.

He said, "Remember the story behind the statement, "Let them eat cake?" He goes into the story very deeply. I couldn't pull up my chair and join them so I'm going to paraphrase what he said.

He states: We all know "Let them eat cake" doesn't mean cake literally. It means brioche/bread. This bread was not the common man's bread. It was a richer bread that the upper class ate and not what the common man ate. Biographers and historians still don't know if that phrase was ever said. But if it was said, the story was of Queen Marie Antoinette supposedly had spoken those words upon hearing how the peasantry had no bread to eat when the

French Revolution was upon them. The statement clearly showed that Marie Antoinette was clueless and oblivious to the conditions of the common man's life.

He continues to say to his date: But if the peasants were able to eat the brioche and not just the poor man's bread, maybe, it could have made those peasants work harder and want more out of life; to have better food, better everything. Now their children never had to eat peasant food again and their lives improved, the quality of their wants and needs all improved because of a loaf of bread.

Ladies, though no one was speaking to me, if I was on that dinner date and he told me that story, that would make my Tasty list!

Tasty: Appreciation/ Knowledge/Bettering oneself.

As that man was buttering his bread, literally! The telling of the story was second to what he was telling his date about himself over a meal.

By using the venues of food as a tool in seeking a mate; whether it's over coffee, cocktails or a meal, everything about your date is right on his plate, at the bar, at the restaurant—Food Talks!

In my story all my food experiences stood in stark contrast to the ingredients I needed in a man for my "Recipe for Love." So the next time you go out with your new beloved date, stay attuned to the chemistry—not just between him and you, but between him and what the food experience is telling you about him.

If I had paid attention to what my food experiences were showing me and listened to what my gut was telling me, "There's something not right Denise," I could have saved myself and my family a great deal of heartache. For me, I spent too much time in relationships that would **never** have worked.

In each relationship we experience, we can taste the flavor of someone's true essence, but we have to dig through the dirt to get to the truffle. Each date or relationship indulgence gets us that much closer to finding the person that is Tasty to our palates.

Ask yourself, "What do I want in a man? What is "Tasty?"

Ask yourself another question, "What don't I want in a man? "Not Tasty?"

Knowing what you <u>don't want</u> is just as important as or more important than knowing what you do want.

When we are only looking for what we want, we set ourselves up to see nothing else. We are a society that wants and that's healthy. It's not healthy to not pay attention to what we don't want, the "Not Tasty."

Example of Denise's Recipe for Love:

<u>Tasty:</u> A man who is aware of himself, who works on his ego and behavior to not always have to be right in a situation. Prefers to be happy than right. That is my # 1 Tasty.

<u>**Not Tasty:**</u> A man who is self-absorbed. This is my # 1 Not Tasty. He can have my # 1 Tasty ingredient and many more from my Tasty list, but that <u>self-absorbed</u> man would be cleared off my plate immediately. I don't care how many Tasty(s) he has. Next!

Chapter Four

Main Entrée

Shiny Penny

*Prince Charming
Has a Secret Ingredient*

I was in my twenties the first time food tried to tell me something about the man I was dating. It was shouting out the ugly truth to me from countless dinner plates the whole time we were together. Each meal spoke to me and after I added them all up, it revealed the entire person. Today, I know how to listen to food from the first dining experience, but back then, I was so naive. This is how my journey with food and men began.

I'd forgotten to grab my grandmother's birthday present. I ran back into my apartment building, grabbed the present and was waiting for the elevator to return as I caught my breath. When the doors opened, I saw a man standing inside; the breath I'd just caught got snatched away.

I'd just had my first look at Shiny Penny.

"Are you going down?" His deep voice was hypnotic. My attraction to him made me self-conscious, awkward and at a loss for words. I walked into the 6-foot-by-4-foot space and was standing directly in front of him. The first thought that went through my mind was, "I hope my ass looks good?"

I got all the necessary information on Shiny Penny in a 20-second elevator ride. Mr. GQ was a 28-year-old model from Los Angeles who had just moved into my apartment building and was living on his own. I didn't want him to be on his own for too long—that wouldn't have been neighborly-like.

When we reached the lobby, I just stood there. Normally, I would have exited quickly, but common sense and I weren't getting along. I waited, hoping Shiny Penny would say something. His mouth opened and I heard him say, "Sleep over?"

In reality, he said, "After you."

Shiny Penny followed me out and stopped at his mailbox. The coast was clear for me to run back to the car like a lunatic where my sister Yvette was waiting. "What is wrong with you?" she asked. I told her I had just met my new boyfriend!

Like Shiny Penny, I too had just moved into that apartment building. After graduating college and working in Boston in the hotel industry for a year, I needed a change. I needed to be home. I moved back to New York City and the energy of Manhattan was like none other, I said goodbye to my hotel career and followed another passion, acting.

New York City was the best date a girl could ever have. Trying to find a man that gave me that same excitement wasn't easy—until the day I laid my eyes on Shiny Penny. I was so mesmerized by Shiny Penny that my mind kept replaying my meeting with him. I couldn't wait to see my new neighbor again.

The following week I was doing my laundry. I put on a hair-dye-stained t-shirt and a pair of ripped jeans, grabbed my clothesbasket and some cut-up watermelon and got into the elevator. I pressed the basement button, but instead of going down, the elevator went two floors up—to the penthouse. The doors opened and in stepped my Shiny Penny. I wanted to die! I visualized dropping my basket, throwing my watermelon in the air and pushing him out on his ass.

"We meet again," he said. I wanted so badly to say, "What do you mean? You've been in my bedroom every night this week." Instead, I offered him some watermelon. Shiny Penny took a few pieces and politely placed the pits from his mouth to his hand. Noticing that I was not doing the same, he asked me if I was eating the pits. "I didn't get any pits in my watermelon," I said, as I swallowed a mouthful.

An awkward silence ensued until Shiny Penny asked me if I wanted to go back up to his apartment for a drink.

"Sure, just give me 10 minutes."

Shiny Penny took my phone number and I waited for his call. I waited and waited. Thirty minutes went by and I had no choice but to have the doorman buzz Shiny Penny's apartment. It turned out that he had fallen asleep and was just about to call me. Thankfully, he wasn't blowing me off. I would have hated to have to move.

After that, Shiny Penny and I dated about two nights a week. We saw plenty of movies, hung out at each other's apartments and I got to know all the coffee houses in the city. Hugs and kisses were sweet, but I needed more action than our PG-rated relationship.

It was time for me to spice things up. I invited Shiny Penny over for a home cooked meal. He told me no woman had ever cooked for him before. "What would you like me to cook for you?" I thought those words out of a woman's mouth would be a song to any man's ears. But Shiny Penny showed no excitement. Instead, he responded like a big lumberjack with his chest pumped out—not his usual soft style. He asked for a hamburger and fries. Burgers were the best he could come up with? Of course he wasn't going to get that. No way was I cooking a diner deluxe order!

The table was set, the candles lit and I was looking for love. When Shiny Penny showed up at my door, he was empty-handed. Not that I expected him to bring me a diamond ring, but flowers or wine would have been nice. We hugged and kissed and his eyes were filled with emotion. I was touched by the look on his face and surprised by his knowledge of my flatware. Yes, Shiny Penny knew more about my plates than I did. At the time, I wrote it off as a cute eccentricity.

I had made a traditional Italian meal: homemade sauce with spaghetti and meatballs. Comfort food was sleepover food. We ate, we talked and yes, we had sex. Not great sex, not good sex, but okay sex. The next morning, I thought I'd try our new sport, sex; again, hoping the second time around would be better. But Shiny Penny told me he was still stuffed from dinner. I had never met a man that was still stuffed from the night before and said no to sex. Hmm?

Over the next five months I made sure we ate light, but a big meal was about to be served the night I was introducing Shiny Penny at my entire family at Easter dinner.

My Aunt Lori's home was filled with family, friends and of course, plenty of food. Platters of our family's recipes filled every inch of the three tables. We gave thanks as everyone held hands. Shiny Penny closed his eyes and embraced the moment as the feeding frenzy began.

As the whole family began talking, eating and passing the food around the table, the volume got louder and louder and then it went silent. It was like an orchestra that had quieted their instruments to allow the singer to sing. The first bar that my Aunt Maryann sung was, "So, Shiny Penny, where is your family today?"

All eyes were now on my boyfriend.

Slowly, Shiny Penny lifted his eyes from his plate. The empty silence made me so nervous that I started to answer for him. Then, he came unwrapped. Right out of the gate Shiny Penny said his parents were divorced, he shared that his mother never had family over and having a family dinner was new to him. He then went on to tell everyone that he only saw his father once in a while and wished he saw more of him. What? Was there truth serum in the food?

I had been with Shiny Penny for six months before learning these intimate details and my family's dinner got them out of him in mere minutes!

After that night, Shiny Penny and I played house. He loved when I cooked dinner for us. He also had another love; bringing the Bible to the dinner table. I was fine with giving thanks for a meal, but putting the Bible on table? I told him there would be no bread dipped in wine being served.

Shiny Penny was okay blessing his meal without the big book, but he decided he wasn't okay with the Big Apple. He moved back to Los Angeles and I went on with my life in New York City. But three weeks later, my own chance to move to L.A. opened up. I was to audition for a prominent L.A.-based improvisational acting school. I took it as a sign that I should be with Shiny Penny. Hollywood, here I come!

The West Coast was beautiful, but I missed my life back home. Since cooking always made me feel better, I had a small dinner party and invited two friends from acting school. I made vegetable lasagna, salad, bread—the works and Shiny Penny baked a coconut pie. Everything was going smoothly until it came time for dessert. I had served the coconut pie on colorful plates. Shiny Penny took one look at the colors and his face clouded with rage. He demanded, in front of our bewildered guests, that the pie be moved to white plates.

Why was he being so anal about a silly dish? He was standing his ground and told me that a man should be able to eat off the dishes he wants. Speechless, I lifted each piece of pie from the colorful plates to the white plates.

After that night, I felt uneasy with Shiny Penny. I bought a bed and furnishings for our second bedroom and moved into it. After you see your boyfriend freak out over colored plates, you need your own space!

I knew I needed a friend to help me get through this. Since all my friends were in New York, it was up to me to make a local new friend, and I did. A native Californian and coincidentally, her name was Denice, just spelt with a "c." When Denice met my boyfriend, she immediately coined the nickname, "Shiny Penny." She thought he tried too hard to perfect his style. Shiny Penny thought it was great that I'd met a new girl friend and it turned out there was another "girl" he wanted me to meet as well: his mother.

We drove to San Francisco to spend the weekend with his mother. She planned an evening in and she was dressed to the town and her voice carried several blocks.

Loud or not, this woman could cook. Her dining table was set beautifully and her kitchen counter was filled with plates of food. The way her food brought her family to the table reminded me of my own family. But in that house, the tension around the table was thicker than gravy.

We sat down to eat in silence. She and I ate heartily, Shiny Penny pushed his food around on his plate. The meal his mother made was delicious. She made Chicken Primavera, a combination of fresh vegetables and chicken sautéed in a broth of garlic and fresh basil. I couldn't understand how Shiny Penny could resist his mother's food. Something was wrong and at the time I was still clueless to what my food experiences were trying to tell me.

I tried to make eye contact with one of them just to get a conversation started. I was searching for something to say, but Shiny Penny's mother beat me to it: "So, my son tells me you two are getting married?"

Before I could fall off my chair, Shiny Penny grabbed my face and started kissing me. "Please, Denise, stay with me on this," he said into my mouth. When he stopped licking my face he told his mother that we were being very private about the details. Really? It must have been very private since he hadn't even told the bride to be—me!

Shiny Penny had never spoke about marriage before. Was he going to propose? Was that why I was meeting his mother? After dinner, I pulled him aside. "Do you have something you want to ask me?"

It's every girl's dream to find her prince—and every girl's nightmare to hear her prince say something that turns him into a frog. Shiny Penny explained that if his mother thought we were getting married she would stay off his back. "What is he talking about?" I thought to myself.

During our visit Shiny Penny's mother made several dishes, each dish better than the last. We enjoyed the food—except Shiny Penny. The entire weekend he just pushed his mother's elegant meals around on his plate.

When we got home, we were cold and quiet towards each other. That night, I moved all my stuff into the second bedroom. During the next few days, we didn't communicate at all, which made the situation more and more uncomfortable. After the fifth night of being apart, I wanted to break the tension between us by surprising Shiny Penny with a home-cooked meal.

Not just any home-cooked meal. I made one of Shiny Penny's mother's recipes: *Beef and Pork Wine Stew*. Now, you might be thinking, why would I make one of his mother's meals when he displayed a dislike for her cooking? I knew his actions had nothing to do with her food. I was hoping that if I made her recipe, he would be able to feel some closeness to his mother without her being in the room.

Shiny Penny glanced at the food. Before he put one bite into his mouth, he asked me what the dish was.

"Surprise! I thought it would be nice to make one of your mother's recipes."

The surprise was on me. He put his fork down and pushed away from the table.

"What? I worked so hard on this meal. You love stews."

"Not my mother's!"

There I was, ready to forgive him and instead of moving back into our bedroom, I just stayed put. I called my father and told him that Shiny Penny and I were not getting along and his behavior odd.

"Relationships are hard, Denise. Give it some time." I gave it some time, but I sensed something was wrong—very wrong. Could he be having an affair and he's acting odd to separate us?

The next morning during breakfast I simply just came right out and asked him. "Are you seeing a woman?"

He replied, "Yes, I'm seeing you." I didn't believe him.

I needed to find out if Shiny Penny was being truthful. The only thing I could think of was to follow him one day, so I did. When Shiny Penny went to the gym, I walked through the front doors right after him. I heard him speaking on his cell phone, "Meet me in front for lunch." When he saw me, he closed his phone.

"What are you doing here Denise?"

"Are you seeing another woman? Tell me the truth."

"I'm not seeing another woman!"

Before I could say anything back to him, I heard Shiny Penny's name called out. I looked into the open gym and saw his trainer, Joe, walking over. Shiny Penny said, "You know my girlfriend, Denise." When Shiny Penny said "girlfriend," I felt relieved.

The next couple of weeks, I did everything I could to make up for pulling away from him. I was caring, playful and didn't cook any of his mother's meals.

Our relationship was getting better and I finished my acting classes in L.A. It was time to go back home to New York City and Shiny Penny was coming home with me. Since I had sublet my New York apartment, I still had my home. When we got to the Big Apple, we were welcomed home by family and friends who prepared a huge feast. Shiny Penny seemed to be enjoying himself, but he also seemed distant.

The next day, Shiny Penny was out visiting friends when he called me and asked me to meet him at one of our favorite restaurants.

When I walked into the restaurant and got closer to the table, Shiny Penny looked very different to me. His appearance was not his normal style. His hair was gelled, his face was scruffy and his shirt was tighter than a Playboy bunny! He was sitting with one of the waiters we knew, and when I said hello, the waiter got up, smiled at me and told Shiny Penny, "Good luck."

Good luck?

"Hi, sweetheart," I said as I sat down next to him.

"Hey, hey." Not the loving greeting I was looking for from him, but I let it slide.

He grabbed my hand and said, "I need to tell you something."

Shiny Penny took a deep breath, told me I was his best friend and how much he loved me, as he was struggling and squirming in his seat. Then he said it:

"I'm gay."

"What did you just say to me?"

"I'm gay."

"What?" I nervously laughed!

"Denise, Denise, I am. I'm gay."

At first I felt lost, hopeless, deceived. Then anger swept over me. "Gay? You're gay?" I kept saying it, "You're gay? What else could I say? Oh please honey, don't be gay.

Food Talks!

Now, years later, I realize that food, tangible or intangible played a major part in showing me that Shiny Penny was hiding something from me. When food was involved, many truths about Shiny Penny's personality were revealed.

Tasty / Not Tasty—The Ingredients of Shiny Penny:

<u>Tasty:</u> When I offered him some watermelon he took a few pieces and politely placed the pits from his mouth to his hand. Ladies, his manners were beyond sexy.

Not Tasty: It took Shiny Penny three weeks to ask me to dinner. Why? He had never asked a girl out to dinner before me.

Tasty: I was the first girl to ever cook for him. Excellent! I had the opportunity to "set the bar."

Not Tasty: The first time I cooked for him he asked for a hamburger. A hamburger? Really? With a lumberjack puffed out chest he was showing me he wasn't comfortable. He told me <u>no woman</u> had ever cooked for him before; again, food was talking. I just figured his past girlfriends didn't know how to cook. Wrong! He had no past girlfriends.

Not Tasty: When he showed up to my apartment for dinner, he was empty handed. Empty handed? That food experience showed me bad manners. Now, I know it was more than that. He wasn't experienced with dining with a woman—you bring her a little something!

Not Tasty: He was to full from dinner the night before to have sex the next morning? More like to full of something else—lies.

Tasty—and now—Not Tasty: A man knowing more about my flatware then I did.

Tasty: When Shiny Penny spoke of his personal life at my family's Easter dinner. The openness and warmth of that dinner allowed Shiny Penny to share some of his family history. For the first time, he was eating with a family that made him feel comfortable.

Not Tasty: At the Easter dinner, there were definite issues with his family that were alluded to over that meal. Shiny Penny and his family were at odds. Perhaps I should have backed off the relationship until he confided in me about his family problems. It seems obvious now that his family knew he was hiding from himself.

Not Tasty: The Bible at the dinner table. I believe in giving thanks, but not out of guilt!

Not Tasty: In Los Angeles, at my dinner party, I must have really been deaf not to hear the coconut pie yelling, "Why am I being transferred to another plate? Eat me already!" Let's face it, when a man gets into a verbal fighting match with his girlfriend over the color of the plates, something is VERY wrong.

Not Tasty: I can't forget the weekend Shiny Penny and I spent at his mother's. The entire time, Shiny Penny pushed his mother's delicious home-cooked meals around on his plate and then he got upset with me for duplicating one of his mother's recipes. Even though his mother might have been a little too over the top for him, she wasn't a mean-spirited woman. If he couldn't respect her enough to eat the food she cooked, there were deeper issues between them.

Not Tasty: To top it off, at his mother's dinner table, Shiny Penny was showing me off as his wife-to-be and expecting me to play along. Obviously, he was hoping to convince his mother her son wasn't gay. I still don't know the whole story, but if I had to guess, Shiny Penny's mother didn't approve of the gay lifestyle.

The ingredients of Shiny Penny could never be on my shopping list, but his mother's recipes could.

Beef & Pork Stew

2 pounds lean stew beef
1-pound pork loin
½ cup virgin olive oil
3 cloves garlic, minced
4 cups of water
2 large cans whole tomatoes
2 thin slices lemon
4 medium onions, sliced in wedges
2 teaspoons salt (to taste)
½ teaspoon pepper (to taste)
10 medium carrots, peeled and cut
7 medium potatoes, quartered
8 fresh basil leaves
2 boxes of frozen peas (2 cups)
1 cup of red wine

In a deep medium size pot, pour virgin olive oil over medium heat, then add beef and pork, add salt and cook for about 10 minutes. After the meat is browned, remove it from the pot and place it aside. Add 2 tablespoons virgin olive oil back into the pot. Place garlic and onions into the skillet and cook until caramelized. Place the meat back into the pot. Add water, lemon slices and the 2 cans of whole tomatoes. Mix well and simmer for 2 hours, turn the meat over occasionally. After 2 hours add carrots, potatoes and red wine. Cover and cook until vegetables are tender (about 30 minutes). Then add frozen peas and fresh basil leaves. Cook until the peas are heated through—about 10 minutes.

Serve hot.

Chicken Primavera

1-pound chicken breast (5-6 cutlets)

½ cup flour

1 can chicken broth

2 cups broccoli florets

2 cups sliced carrots

2 cups fresh mushrooms

1 package of frozen peas (1 cup)

¼ cup virgin olive oil

2 cups fresh diced plum tomatoes

2 cloves garlic, minced

1 small onion, diced

3 leaves fresh basil

½ cup minced fresh parsley

½-1 cup light cream (to taste)

½-1 cup freshly grated Parmesan cheese (to taste)

Salt and pepper (to taste)

Flour the chicken lightly. In a skillet pan over medium heat, pour in olive oil. Brown the chicken on each side—2 minutes. Remove the chicken from the skillet and place on the side. Add 2 more tablespoons of olive oil to the skillet.

Add onions and garlic and cook until caramelized. Stir in the chicken broth, let that simmer for 5 minutes and stir in the light cream. Keep stirring the combined liquids for 10 minutes. Place the chicken back into the skillet and add the broccoli, carrots, mushrooms and fresh parsley. Simmer for 20 minutes. Then add the frozen peas, fresh tomatoes, basil and Parmesan cheese. Simmer for 20 minutes before serving.

Serve hot.

Shrimp Scampi
with Cherry Tomatoes

1 pound jumbo shrimp, shelled and de-veined

4 cloves minced garlic

1 tablespoon of butter

½ cup of dry white wine

2 medium lemons

2 tablespoons of finely chopped flat-leaf parsley leaves

1½-cups of cherry tomatoes

½ cup of olive oil

Red pepper flakes (a few dashes)

Salt and pepper (to taste)

Wash the shrimp in cold water. Drain and place the shrimp in a large dish.

Completely dry the shrimp with paper towels. Heat a large skillet pan over medium heat. Add butter and olive oil. Add garlic and sautéed for 5 minutes. Place the shrimp into the skillet and cook the shrimp for 5 minutes. Remove the shrimp from the skillet into a bowl. Place aside.

Return the skillet over medium heat and add white wine, lemon juice, parsley and cherry tomatoes, cook for about 20 minutes. Pour the shrimp back into the skillet, add salt and pepper to taste and a few dashes of red pepper flakes. Toss to combine.

Serve hot.

Pasta with Tomato & Basil Sauce

1-pound pasta (penne, spaghetti)

¼ cup pine nuts, toasted

1-pint cherry tomatoes (cut into halves)

3 cloves garlic, minced

1-teaspoon red pepper flakes (to taste)

½ cup basil leaves, torn

½ cup olive oil

½ cup of chicken broth (or vegetable broth)

½ cup of fresh grated Parmesan cheese

Salt and pepper (to taste)

In a medium sauté pan over medium-high heat, toast the pine nuts until golden brown, about 3 minutes, set aside. Place the pan back on the stove over medium-high heat and add the olive oil and sauté garlic, 5 minutes. Add tomatoes and let simmer for 30 minutes. Add the broth, the red pepper flakes and the basil to the pan. Cook for another 30 minutes then remove sauce from the heat.

Boil water in large pot and add pasta. Cook according to package directions—about 10 minutes. Drain the pasta then put back into the large pot. Toss the pasta with salt and pepper and a touch more of olive oil. Top the pasta with the tomato and basil sauce. When plating, sprinkle the toasted pine nuts over the pasta and add Parmesan cheese.

Serve hot.

Penne Sautéed with
Zucchini & Onions

1-pound penne pasta

½ cup olive

4 cups zucchini, (2 large zucchini), diced

2 cloves of garlic (chopped)

1 can of chicken or vegetable broth

1 cup grated Parmesan cheese

Salt and pepper (to taste)

In a large skillet pan, simmer olive oil for about 1 minute until hot. Add the diced onion and sauté until golden, about 5-10 minutes then add garlic. Add the zucchini and cook until the zucchini starts to brown and soften, about 10 minutes add the broth and simmer on low heat for 20 minutes.

Boil water in a large pot and add pasta. Cook according to package directions, about 10 minutes. Drain the pasta. Add the pasta to the skillet of broth, zucchini and onions and add the grated cheese. Toss and plate. Season with salt and pepper, add more cheese to taste.

Serve hot.

Chapter Five

Main Entrée
Rockefeller

Dinner and a Show

"Would you like me to introduce you?" My father asked.

"Absolutely not!"

It was a Saturday spring night and I was having dinner with my father at a New York City SOHO restaurant we frequented. As our coffee was served, my father called my attention to the fact that a man who was also dining, who my father knew of, was more interested in me than the appetizers on his table. Yes, I was guilty of looking over at the man, but that didn't mean I was ordering him for dessert.

It had been months since my breakup with Shiny Penny but dating and relationships were the last things I wanted to think about. My guard was up and I had become way too direct towards the opposite sex. My social skills were horrific. It didn't matter where I was; if a man approached me, my first question to him was, "Are you gay?" Some men thought my question was a joke. Little did they know there was no punch line.

At first, when Shiny Penny and I broke up, I did say yes to a couple of dinner date invitations. Without fail, on each date I found myself talking to the restaurants' bathroom mirrors. "Why did I say yes to this date? Did I meet him at a petting zoo? I don't remember being asked out by a jackass!"

It wasn't the men's fault. It was me. Could you blame me? I was still getting over the fact that my first real adult boyfriend, with whom I'd spent two years of my life with, turned out to prefer men!

My biggest fear about getting into another relationship was the fact that I would have to trust someone again. All the factors involved in starting all over again—they didn't just exhaust me, they freaked me out!

Then, on that one Saturday spring night, something changed. The man in the restaurant didn't catch my eye because of his physical status. This man possessed a grand powerful magnetic energy. He was a distinguished older man with a regal sparkling star-presence that would intrigue anyone. If he were an actor in a Broadway show, he would be playing the role of the main character, "Rockefeller."

I had never seen a man who received so much attention. When Rockefeller spoke to the waiters they ran to him as if he were their King. They kept serving his table plates of food and bottles of wine. Even the friends dining with him were fawning over him. It was more than a feast; it was a royal fiesta!

As enticing as Rockefeller was, I still wasn't ready to meet anyone. So what was I doing looking over at him? My mind said yes, but my heart said, don't be crazy!

"Are you sure you don't want me to introduce you?" My father said once again.

"No, I was just looking. Let's get the check."

I told my father I appreciated the fact that he was encouraging me to date again, but begged him to please stop trying. As I was explaining why, my father raised his eyebrows, trying to signal me that you-know-who was coming up right behind me—time to shut it. I paid no attention to my father. Unfortunately, I just kept talking until Rockefeller extended his arm across the table and in the midst of my ramble, he said, "Hello, Richard, this must be one of your daughters." Forget the foot; my whole damn leg was in my mouth. I pronounced a slow, drawn out "H-E-L-L-O." Rockefeller must have thought I had a speech impediment.

I had to think fast. I had to get out of that situation. So I did what needed to be done. I lied. "I'm so sorry, but I need to excuse myself, I have to go home." Rockefeller must have thought I was the rudest person in the world, but my father knew exactly what I was doing: panicking!

Three weeks later, I found myself back at that same SOHO restaurant. As I was walking in, Rockefeller was walking out. He'd been the farthest thing from my mind and the last person I'd expected to see again. There we were, eyeball to eyeball. We greeted each other with an uncomfortable "hey," and then Rockefeller said, "Well, have a good night, Denise." Before I could say anything back to him, a handful of people right behind him bombarded me. Rockefeller's entourage followed his every step. My God, does this guy always dine with an army of people? Two minutes after I saw Rockefeller, he was out of my thoughts.

I bumped into him again the following week at a dinner party I attended with my father. If my father hadn't known him, I would have sworn he was stalking me. I couldn't believe that in a period of five weeks, I'd seen Rockefeller three times. How could this keep happening in a city with millions of people?

"Having a good time, Denise?" Again, Rockefeller remembered my name. I was impressed but not sold. I decided to give the poor guy a break and invited him to sit at my table. I was giving Rockefeller one shot and one shot only. Of course, as soon as Rockefeller sat next to me, several of the other party guests interrupted us. Hadn't these people heard of bad timing?

Within a few minutes a crowd of people had gathered around us or should I say, around him. Rockefeller politely asked whether I minded if he spoke with his friends for a moment. Perfect! It gave me a chance to find my father and get the scoop.

"Quickly, Dad, tell me what you know about Rockefeller." My father didn't really know much about him, except that Rockefeller was a well-known customer at that SOHO restaurant. They had bumped into each other there on occasion and when they did, they shared some small talk.

My father thought Rockefeller was a gentleman, and knew he was in his mid-thirties who lived in New Jersey and owned an Italian restaurant. *Molto bene!*

Even with all the 411 information I had just heard, I was still hoping that when Rockefeller returned to my table, he would crash and burn. I was adamant about not dating, but Rockefeller and I got along tremendously. Damn it!

"I'll see you tomorrow night at eight o'clock, Denise for dinner." Rockefeller said as he dropped me off later that night. He didn't even ask me for my phone number. Was he afraid I might cancel or was this a sign of arrogance?

Buzz! It was eight o'clock sharp the next night and I had yet to put my face on. Rockefeller was right on time. Didn't he know he should always give a girl an extra 10 minutes? Now I had a new question: Hadn't he ever gone on a date before or was he a control freak?

On to the date, which turned out to be a gluttonous banquet, Rockefeller must have ordered one of everything off the menu and then some. One glance at him and I quickly surmised that he must work out three hours a day. Too bad I didn't. Next dress size up please!

I quickly got an answer to one of my question: yes, he was controlling. I'd expected him to order the wine, but I hadn't expected him to order all the food. Rockefeller didn't even let my hands touch the menu. He even instructed me regarding the order in which I should taste everything. Apparently this was very important to the multi-dish feasting experience—he said, he knew best. That gave me the answer to the other question: yes, he was arrogant, but in an attractive way. Every move he made was with such graciousness, politeness and savoir-faire that I didn't mind. Rockefeller did know his food; after all, he owns a restaurant.

As I was eating, I started to feel like I was with a great dancer who was whisking me around on the dance floor in a heated tango. In that moment, I thought, what would Rockefeller be like in bed? He was successful, charming and very aware of his appearance with a light sense of humor. The best part was he wasn't so arrogant that he couldn't laugh at himself when I was being a smartass. "Did your manicure come with this dinner?" You know ladies, just to say something to keep him on his toes.

I was suddenly struck by another thought. What would Rockefeller be like in a relationship? I was so overwhelmed by the restaurant, the food and let's not forget my sexual thoughts—I forgot there were other people around us.

Over dinner, Rockefeller's conversation was basic; it never got too deep. He talked about how nice it was to see each other again, how beautiful the night was. I was just going with the flow, following his lead. I didn't want the night to end, but surprisingly, Rockefeller ended the evening with a gentle peck on my cheek. He was so sure that I would see him again that he said, "I'll see you tomorrow at eight."

I replied, "I can't wait!"

Over the next few months, we saw each other every moment we could. After a month, I got an answer to my question about what he'd be like in bed. I also got to find out the answer to my other question, what he'd be like in a relationship. The answer was the same for both. Wow!

I just wished he could have be more comfortable with just me. I wanted to be with him without having to be part of the big show, restaurant after restaurant.

My kitchen was lonely; I hadn't cooked in nine months. We never ate in. Every night was another big to-do. In all those months, we had never stayed home and had a home-cooked meal and watched a video in our sweats. I planned a night for us at my apartment, wanting to show him that I too can make us dinner without a Chef! What I really wanted was some alone time with intimate conversation, just for the two of us.

When Rockefeller came over that night, he wasn't alone. He had invited two other couples. Not only did he disregard my plans, he'd gone food shopping and was making the meal that night, a huge roasted lamb dinner.

Rockefeller wouldn't let me do anything. I wasn't even allowed in my own kitchen. What made it worse was that he was so consumed with making, serving and eating the food that he didn't even notice that I was giving him the silent treatment.

The next morning, Rockefeller woke up, kissed me good-bye and drove back to his home. I didn't say anything to him right then and there, but the next night at dinner I did. Face to face, I told Rockefeller straight up that I was sick of going out and I was tired of having the spotlight on us every night.

Rockefeller replied, "I would love to spend next weekend alone with you." All week I dreamed of being wonderfully alone with my boyfriend. Well, that dream ended on Thursday. Rockefeller called me, said he had totally forgotten that his parents were coming in from Florida. Bye-bye quiet weekend. Almost a year of being together and we still hadn't had any real alone time.

"This is way too much!" Rockefeller's mother said when she saw all the food the servers were bringing to the table. Yes, we were dining out again and the restaurant had a four star rating. Not only was his mother uncomfortable with the food, she was uncomfortable with the prices. Rockefeller's father didn't have any reaction, but his mother was ill at ease in the surroundings. It was clear that since she hadn't seen her son in over a year, she too would have preferred to have a more intimate evening at his home. It was nice to know I wasn't the only one who thought "grand" wasn't always necessary.

"Mom, please, can you just enjoy your dinner?" Rockefeller's mother was a simple, down-to-earth woman and even though she was dressed nicely, she wore simple clothes with an understated style. The restaurant and its' customers were far from simple: Chanel, Gucci, Armani, definitely not his mother's scene. Rockefeller's father again had no reaction and couldn't talk with all the food he was chewing.

The stew got thicker once his mother said, "I don't even know what I'm eating." You should have seen Rockefeller's facial expression. It wasn't pretty, but it was nothing compared to when his father said, "I think it's some kind of fish."

Rockefeller was about to respond in a way that I knew we would all regret. I immediately turned toward his mother and said, "So, do you like to cook?" I had no idea if she did or didn't. I quickly mentioned that I loved cooking, but ever since I've met her son, I never get the chance to cook anymore. Yes, that side bar of information was meant for Rockefeller to hear. Hint, hint!

Oh boy, did I open up a can of worms! She let me know what she cooked, how she cooked and she insisted that I even write down her number one ingredient in every meal, TLC—Tender Loving Care. She served a weekly menu of home-cooked meals; Monday night meatloaf to Friday night pizza. The recipes she spoke of were very easy dishes, nothing too fancy, not expensive, just simple everyday meals. The way she described her cooking made me want to get up and run to my kitchen – I missed cooking myself a home cooked meal! Her philosophy was simple, inexpensive, but tasty and healthy.

How could a simple woman produce a showman like Rockefeller? Was he adopted? Rockefeller wasn't so happy with me after that dinner because I was agreeing with his mother that the restaurant was a bit much. The following week was long. I suffered through Rockefeller's distant and cold attitude but I continued to push the envelope and demanded our weekend alone.

I was optimistic. I mean, it was going to be the first time we were dining together without another person in the room. I was so excited that I had Rockefeller all to myself; all I wanted was for us to talk with each other. I was hungry for real conversation.

The night before our first "alone" dinner, I decided what I was going to cook. I thought about what Rockefeller's mother had said, "Simple." If I spent less time in the kitchen and cooked an easy yet tasty meal, then Rockefeller and I would spend more time together.

I made his mother's meatloaf with a leaf-only salad and bought some bread from the local deli. You might be thinking, this was your first time cooking for your boyfriend and you couldn't do better than meatloaf? But that dinner was not meant to be fancy; it was about me showing Rockefeller how simplicity is needed in a relationship.

Unfortunately, it was too simple for Rockefeller. He started asking me if I made any vegetables and potatoes and how come I didn't add tomatoes to the salad. Everything I didn't do for that meal was to make more time for us together.

Throughout our relationship, we were constantly out at restaurants and surrounded by people. When the show was on, Rockefeller's control and arrogance came across as charming, but when it was just the two of us, off stage, all the charm faded.

I wasn't sure if I wanted this relationship anymore. Yet, as fast as that thought flew through my mind, I threw it right back out. Monday came and I decided to call Rockefeller and just say, "I love you." But before I got a chance, Rockefeller said, "Denise, we need to talk."

What? Are you kidding me? There I was, going to stay and work on our relationship, and *I'm* getting the boot?

Months later, February was now upon us and I had no Valentine. On my way out that night to join my other single friends for a Valentine's dinner, my home phone rang and the caller ID flashed, there was Rockefeller's name in lights. I took a deep breath and answered with a calm hello. It was silent on the other end. Again I said, "Hello?" For a few seconds I heard nothing and then I heard Rockefeller say,

"Oh no…Denise, I meant to dial 411 for information to get a phone number to a restaurant."

That was all I needed to hear. Rockefeller: Over!

Food Talks!

When it came to Rockefeller, food was pulling back the curtain for me to really see the actor before the man.

Tasty / Not Tasty—The Ingredients of Rockefeller:

Tasty: The first time I set eyes on Rockefeller, everything around him was entertaining, lots of friends, lots of food, seemed like a great deal of fun. No wonder he got my attention. It was dinner and a show.

Not Tasty: When I bumped into him the second time at the restaurant, he walked out the front door and so did his entourage right behind him. Rockefeller liked a great deal of attention—I didn't!

Tasty: On our first date, he ordered the meal, the wine and the dessert without ever letting me look at the menu. Ladies, to me, I love when a man knows how to order a meal. Being a gentle alpha male is attractive to me.

Not Tasty: Yes, I liked his style of ordering, but his instruction on what to eat first was a bit much. It wasn't like I was ordering dessert as an appetizer. It's not attractive to me when someone I *just* met tells me what to do. Let me ask first.

Tasty: The food told me something else about Rockefeller. What he was like at the table gave me a glimpse of how he'd be in bed, hungry. Letting Rockefeller take control of the meal and slowly savoring every taste, I came to believe that he would savor me and satisfy my hunger in a relationship.

<u>Tasty:</u> Rockefeller knew the secret to romance, the foreplay *was* the meal. I was hooked, caught and reeled in.

Not Tasty: My sexual appetite took over. The food was talking, but I had stopped listening. With Rockefeller, my instincts got lost in my sexual attraction. We were only in the middle of our first meal, still in general conversation, when I made up my mind about a future with him. I never got to a deeper conversation. Now I see that there were so many dishes crammed on our table that Rockefeller could only sample each dish, never savoring any of them. He never allowed himself to know any of those dishes completely—just like he never got to know me and never let me know him completely.

Not Tasty: Even almost a year into our relationship, Rockefeller and I had still never shared a quiet meal at home. All the restaurants, all the served meals and all the different dishes kept me entertained and preoccupied. The show distracted me enough so that I couldn't hear what the food was telling me. The food was the main attraction, **not me!** Now I can see that the meals were the only thing Rockefeller and I really shared. I might as well have been dating the food.

Not Tasty: When I met his mother, some of the truth of who he was came out. I was dating a character, not the man. Rockefeller was really a simple, middle class guy with humble beginnings, much like his mother. The food was telling me that in his attempt to attract upscale clientele to his restaurant, he'd had to forget where he came from—to forget the simple man he really was. The audience in the front row wanted to see Rockefeller. I just wish he had given me a backstage pass.

<u>Not Tasty:</u> By the time I'd finally had enough and demanded to spend alone time with him, it was too late. We should have gotten to a "deeper conversation" over dessert on that first date, not a year later. That last weekend should have been our first. Once again, if I had only listened to the food, I would have realized that Rockefeller and I were never going to be able share the stage together.

When you're in the mood for simple, honest home-cooking, enjoy Rockefeller's mother's recipes.

Rockefeller's Mother's Recipes
Homemade Pizza

1 ingredient (TLC) Tender Loving Care

Homemade Tomato Sauce
1 can of tomatoes (16.oz can)
½ cup of virgin olive oil
1 medium onion
2 cloves of garlic
½ cup of freshly grated Parmesan cheese
1½ cups of grated mozzarella
Salt and pepper (to taste)

Dough
¼ cup warm water
1 envelope active dry yeast
1-teaspoon sugar
4 cups bread flour
½ teaspoon salt
1¼ cups cold water
1 tablespoon olive oil

Homemade Tomato Sauce:

Heat a medium size saucepan over low-medium heat. Pour in olive oil. Heat for about 2 minutes; add onion and sauté until translucent. Add garlic, salt and pepper. Stir together for 3 minutes (don't burn the garlic). Pour in the can of tomatoes. Simmer over low heat for 1 hour.

Dough Mixture:

In a bowl, combine warm water, yeast, and sugar. Stir with a spoon to combine. In a separate bowl, mix flour with salt. Then add the envelope of yeast, cold water and oil to flour and salt. Using your hands, knead the flour mixture together until a ball is formed (you can also use a food processor). Remove the dough out of the bowl and place onto a lightly floured counter or wood cutting board and knead for 10 minutes until dough is smooth. Allow the dough to rest for 2 to 3 minutes. Lightly oil a bowl and place the dough into the bowl. Cover with a cloth and let the dough rise at room temperature for 1 hour.

Remove the cloth and push down on the dough and remove it from the bowl. Spilt the dough into 2 to 4 balls and let rise another 30 minutes.

Preheat the oven to 400 degrees. Form all of the dough in a 10 to 12 inch pan (round or square). Spread tomato sauce on the dough and top with grated mozzarella. Place your choice of any other toppings on the dough and place the pizza in the oven. Bake until golden, about 15 to 20 minutes. Top with grated Parmesan cheese. Set aside for 5 minutes then serve.

Serve hot.

Escarole with Pine Nuts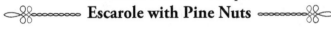

(TLC)
1 head of escarole
½ cup of extra-virgin olive oil
2 cloves garlic (chopped)
½ cup of pine nuts
Red pepper flakes (optional)
Salt and pepper (to taste)

Separate the escarole leaves and rinse thoroughly in warm water and salt. In a large pot bring 3 quarts of water to a boil. Place the escarole leaves into the boiling water. Do not cover. (Covering will dull crisp green color). Cook until tender, about 15 minutes.

When the escarole is tender, drain thoroughly and let dry. Roughly chop the escarole. In a medium size skillet, heat the olive oil until hot. Add the pine nuts. Once pine nuts are toasted, add in garlic, escarole and sauté for 10 minutes. Add red pepper flakes (optional) stir for 5 minutes. Remove from the heat and serve.

Serve hot or room temperature.

Mamma's Meatloaf

(TLC)

½ pound ground pork

½ pound ground veal

1 pound ground beef

2 tablespoons vegetable oil

½ cup of breadcrumbs

1 medium yellow onion, diced

1 clove garlic

1 celery stalk, diced

1 carrot, diced

½ cup flat-leaf parsley

1 large egg

½ cup tomato sauce or ketchup

2 teaspoons mustard (mild)

1 tablespoon salt

1 teaspoons of black pepper

Preheat oven to 375 degrees.

In a medium bowl add breadcrumbs, pork, veal and ground beef. In a medium-size saucepan over medium heat, add oil. Add onion, garlic, celery, carrots and parsley. Sauté until vegetables soften. Add the sautéed vegetables to the meat, along with the egg, tomato sauce or ketchup, mustard and salt and pepper.

Using your hands to mix well, combine thoroughly. Mold the meat into a loaf. Place the meat in a deep-dish pan or loaf pan. Place the meatloaf in the oven and cook for 45 minutes.

Serve hot.

Split Pea Soup
with Ham

(TLC)

1 pound green split peas (frozen)

½ pound smoked or plain ham (diced)

½ cup vegetable oil

3 cloves of garlic

1 large onion (chopped)

2 celery stalks (chopped)

2 large carrots (chopped)

1 cup of parsley

4 sprigs fresh thyme

1 bay leaf

8 cups of chicken stock (4 cans)

1 tablespoon of salt (more for taste)

Salt and pepper (to taste)

Pour oil into a large soup pot over medium heat. Heat the oil for about 1 minute. Add onions, garlic, celery and carrots and sauté until vegetables soften, 10 minutes. Add the parsley, thyme and bay leaf. Add the peas to the pot of ingredients and stir for 10 minutes. Add the chicken stock, salt and pepper. Lower the heat to a simmer, cover and cook for 30 minutes. Remove the pot from the stove. Let cool.

Puree the soup with a hand-held blender or pour into a blender. When the soup is blended, pour back into the pot, add the diced ham and cook over low heat. Simmer for another 20 minutes. Pour soup into soup bowls and add salt and pepper to taste.

Serve hot.

Rockefeller's Mother's Recipes
Swiss Cheese Quiche
with Spinach

(TLC)

6 eggs

1 cup light cream or half-and-half

¼ cup real mayonnaise

2 tablespoons sour cream

2 tablespoons flour

½ cup of minced onions

1 teaspoon garlic powder

8 ounces shredded Swiss cheese

1 small package fresh spinach (chopped) or frozen (defrost)

1 (9-inch) unbaked pie shell (store bought)

Salt and pepper (to taste)

Preheat the oven to 350 degrees.

In a medium bowl with a fork, hand-whip the eggs, cream or half-and-half, mayonnaise, sour cream. Add onions, garlic powder, Swiss cheese and spinach and mix thoroughly. Pour into an unbaked 9-inch, deep piecrust. Place pie mixture in the oven and bake for 45 minutes to 1 hour or until the top is golden brown.

Set aside for 10 minutes before serving.

Chapter Six

Main Entrée

Poppy

*Too Much Spice Will
Give You a Hangover*

After the last two ex-boyfriend disasters, I decided to embrace Cindy Lauper's philosophy, "Girls just want to have fun." I became a wild, free spirited woman just doing her thing. Keeping myself in shape and healthy. The only problem—I was bored to death!

I was in a rut and missing men! A relationship was not what I had in mind; I just wanted some fun-some casual dating. I started being more social and got back into the single scene. Going out to laugh, eat, drink and looking for Mr. Now!

It was a Friday night, my plans were to go out to dinner with my best friend Annie and go home early, but that didn't happen. The adventures of the night grabbed us and the next thing we knew, we were hitting New York City's nightclub scene.

Lights, camera, action!

Annie and I danced our way into a trendy downtown spot. The lights, the loud music and the crowd were blinding. As we stood next to the bar, Annie leaned her body up against mine so I could hear what she was saying.

All eyes were now on us. One set of eyes belonged to "Poppy." His first words to me were, "Can I buy you a drink or would you just prefer the cash?"

It was one of the funniest pickup lines I had ever heard. He was a 37-year old Interior Designer, Latino from Texas who had been living in New York City for the past 12 years. We spoke for an hour and then shared an innocent kiss. Ok, we had an intense make–out session in public. Poppy was all I needed to get myself back into the groove of dating. He wet my appetite to date again.

Poppy wanted to see me again and his plans were to come by my place for some wine later in the week. My plans were – *you're taking me out on a dinner date!* A few days later, he cancelled. The guy calls me, makes plans and then cancels. Unbelievable!

A few weeks later I passed him on the street. Poppy neglected to tell me that he lived literally one block away from me.

"Denise, let me make it up to you?"

"No thank you!" That was all I could say to be polite.

I wasn't interested in getting blown off again; however, his make-up invitation was the finest dinner invite an art lover could ask for. He invited me to a black-tie event at The Museum of Art. I couldn't resist, yes!

The event was breathtaking. Sitting to my right was Poppy and directly next to him was a famous theatrical actor. We were in the company of talent, intellect and gracious guests. I was in heaven. As we were being served dinner, I overheard Poppy speaking with the actor. He was telling the very famous gentleman that he had graduated college with a degree in Cosmopolitan Beauty and had his own hair salon.

"I would love to style your hair for your next film," Poppy so convincingly said.

What the hell was going on here? Wasn't Poppy an Interior Designer? Did he think it was funny to lie about his career?

After that night, I learned very quickly that Poppy was a big joker. He made up elaborate tales during dinner parties, which people actually believed all the time. He had to be the one who was talking; he wasn't letting anyone else ask him anything about himself. He was fun and I was just having a good time with him.

While I was just having a good time with Poppy, I was unaware that he had developed strong feelings for me. How could I possibly know? Life was one big joke with him, until he surprised me with a reservation at a fancy restaurant. Out of the clear blue, his punch lines disappeared and things turned serious. He professed his love, very loudly, in front of the entire restaurant. "I love you! I'm in love with you Denise!"

To say I was surprised would be an understatement. For once, the comedian in Poppy wasn't trying to get a laugh. He was trying to get my love. He had no fear, didn't care what anyone thought. More importantly for *him,* he didn't seem to be interested in what I thought or felt. As soon as he released his emotion, he grabbed the waiter, asked for champagne and looked at the menu. Poppy was just fine with my silence. I wasn't being silent on purpose. Was I ready to have a relationship with the funny man who wasn't joking around anymore? He was serious about us—I just needed to get on board.

After that night, Poppy went right back into his "stand-up" routine and he was drinking and eating and drinking some more—over and over again. I used to ask him to take us to the hottest place in the city—AA!

Poppy told me he was going through some financial challenges so I started picking up the check here and there. I had no problem sharing our food and drink expenses, but he was becoming too expensive for me. I thought he had a great job and made a comfortable living. Where was he spending all his money? Soon, the occasional check that I picked up became the norm. I was now bankrolling our bellies.

Enough was enough. I was making a change—no more going out to eat, I was ready for a quiet dinner at my apartment, just a meal between two people who were dating.

Steak and potatoes were on my menu, a Texan man's dream dinner. My idea was to keep his mouth full of food so that the wine would be limited. That night as I was cooking dinner, my door swung open at 7:00 pm. Poppy was never late for a meal, "Hi honey, I'm home." He used to say every time he came over my apartment. He needed new material, but that night was not the night for me to become his comic writer.

As we ate, I tried to have a conversation, but I was constantly interrupted by his grunts of approval. "Yummy, mmmm." Yes, he liked my cooking, that was obvious. I received high praise when he compared my cooking to his mother's. "This dinner reminds me of being home with my mother." He went on to tell me how his mother cooked every day and he never could get enough of her food.

Poppy's mother's meals were a love affair unto themselves, a true testament to the unconditional love he felt from her. He was an adult with adult responsibilities yet he still craved the love he felt when he ate his mother's food. Those memories of his mother showing him love though food were one of the doorways into his heart. He spoke of his favorite dishes she would make and how he would help her in the kitchen with the family's recipes. Of course I related!

The "mom" door was now opened and I wanted to know more about his relationship with her. All Poppy could do was smile from ear to ear as he spoke of her. It was a tender moment for me to see how a man loved his mother so such that he actually started to choke up as he was speaking of her.

He went on to tell me how she made dinner every night so the family could sit down as one. She kept his family together. She wanted her sons and their father to have a close bond. I asked about his friendships and past Texan sweethearts. All he said was, "You're my sweetheart." Unfortunately, I wasn't feeling the same. Something was missing. Could it be intimacy?

We were together constantly. I brought Poppy to every family dinner and he was the entertainment. One liners and funny stories were his "M.O." He loved all my relatives, especially the children. At one of my family's dinners, he asked for us to sit at the kids table. He would say, "I love children! I miss kids around me." Hmm?

After all the time Poppy spent at my family dinners and us being together for eight months, word came, The Texan's were coming! Poppy's male cousins were invading NYC. It was going to be Texas style. Big!

This was going to be my first encounter with Poppy's family. They were going to do big shopping, big buying and big dinners! His cousins were staying the weekend and the first night they arrived I wasn't invited to dinner. I was sure that Poppy just wanted to spend some time catching up with his family without me. There was always Saturday and Sunday night for him to introduce me, right?

Sunday morning came and I was still on my own. How could Poppy not want me around the entire weekend? He always wanted me by his side—now his family was here and he forgets he has a girlfriend? Well, I was going to dinner Sunday night. I invited myself New York style. Bold!

Soon I was dressed and walking out my door to meet them at the restaurant.

When I arrived I could see something was weighing heavily on Poppy's heart. His cousins were lovely towards me—yet quite.

A week later Poppy lost his job. He was out of control and drinking his worries away. He had nothing—but me.

What was eating at Poppy?

I supported my boyfriend as much as I could. I made breakfast, lunch and dinner—we danced at home, listened to music and I tried to take the pressure off of him. I was doing everything *just for him*.

I encouraged him to call his mother. I knew she would lift his spirits. I never got to meet her in person, but we spoke that night and several times after. She always told me how she prayed for her son to find a nice girl. The pressure was on. As much as I loved Poppy, how could I marry a man who was already engaged to his cocktail?

One night at dinner, I had had enough and I was going to tell him that we needed to take a break. I couldn't support him or this behavior anymore. Before I could utter a word, he came clean.

"There are two little girls that call me Daddy."

There it was, out in the open, the pain that was causing Poppy to joke and drink himself out of his pain.

Poppy went on to tell me that 5 years ago he had two little girls with his past girlfriend, who, at the time, lived in New York City with him. Suddenly and without warning, 3 years ago she moved back to Texas and disappeared without a trace.

He went on to tell me that just over the past year the mother of his children had made contact with him and he was happily financially supporting his children. He cried as he explained how for the past 3 years he had been looking for his two little girls without success.

To me all that mattered was that those children knew who their father was. That meant Poppy leaving New York and going to Texas. Now that was something I wanted to support!

The constant joking and drinking over every meal was Poppy's way of not having to deal with his pain of losing his children.

Food Talks!
Coffee, cocktails or a meal—In Poppy's case, it was one out of three that spoke the loudest.

Tasty / Not Tasty—The Ingredients of Poppy:
<u>Tasty:</u> From the minute Poppy walked up to me in the nightclub with his one liner, I laughed. Laughter is very attractive to me when it comes to my "Recipe for Love."

Not Tasty: Poppy didn't ask me out on a date; he asked to come over to my apartment and bring over some wine. Booty Call – Wrong girl!

Not Tasty: I suggested that we go out on a dinner date. Poppy said yes and then cancelled on me. Cancelling a first real date with someone is just rude.

<u>Tasty:</u> Seeing each other on the street Poppy *immediately* wanted to make up for cancelling our first date. His invitation to join him at the Museum dinner was going to be an incredible evening to experience. Make up sex isn't always the way to go.

Not Tasty: At the Museum dinner, he couldn't be himself. Yes, I like a good joke, but now I see his joking was his way of avoid his "real" life.

<u>Tasty:</u> Poppy was able to shout out "I love you!" In a restaurant filled with customers. He had no fear; he was confident.

Not Tasty: I never said a word to him as he celebrated his love for me. He wasn't thinking of me, he was creating some joy in his life; whether I was on board or not.

Not Tasty: I was paying for most of our dates. At that time I didn't know Poppy was supporting his children. Those food and drink experiences were telling me that there was a reason he couldn't treat me to a night out. He wasn't ready to tell me and I never asked.

Not Tasty: Constant eating, drinking and joking. Maybe if I wasn't drunk, full and always entertained, I would have paid attention to what was eating at him!

<u>Tasty:</u> The dinner I cooked for him was a tender night. I sparked a memory for him and he shared with me how he loved his mother and appreciated all her efforts to keep his family together. A man who loves his mother is one of the main ingredients to my heart.

Not Tasty: After Poppy expressed his love for his mother's family dinners in Texas, he wouldn't say anything about his past loves in Texas when I asked; he didn't say one word, but his body language spoke volumes over that meal—something was not right.

Not Tasty: He didn't invite me to meet his cousins when they came to the city, I had to invite myself. He didn't want his family to misspeak and talk about his children.

<u>Tasty:</u> At my family's dinner everyone loved being around him and he loved being with them, especially the children. Even though I didn't know he had children of his own at the time, he showed me he would make a great father. Family dinners speak volumes about a person.

Not Tasty: I take full responsibility for trying too hard to make him happy. I let the friendship take over the relationship and I forgot about myself. I wasn't listening to the food and drink experiences that screamed at me that Poppy was filling up an empty heart. I spent a year and a half of my life not listening to the over indulging drinking that numbed Poppy's pain filled heart. I couldn't make him happy—he needed to do that on his own.

Rice and Beans

2 cups of chicken broth (store bought)

1 cup enriched white rice

2 tablespoons of vegetable oil

1 medium onion, chopped

1 cup red pepper (diced)

1 can of red kidney beans, drained

1 tablespoon of cayenne pepper or hot sauce (to taste)

2 tablespoons of rice vinegar

Salt and pepper (to taste)

In a medium saucepan over medium heat bring chicken broth to a boil. Add white rice, lower heat and cover. Simmer rice for 20 minutes and then stir the rice. When rice is done, remove it from the stovetop.

In a medium skillet over medium-high heat, add vegetable oil, onions and red peppers. Cook for 10 minutes to soften. Add beans to the mixture, stir in the cayenne pepper or hot sauce and the rice vinegar. Simmer the beans over low heat for 10 minutes. Put the beans on top of the rice and serve. Season rice and beans with salt and pepper to taste.

Serve hot.

Chicken Enchiladas

1 pound of chicken cutlets (shredded)
10 flour tortillas (soft)
½ cup of vegetable oil
¼ cup of chili powder
2 cups of chicken stock
1 small can of tomato puree (or cup)
3 cups of grated cheddar cheese
1 onion medium (chopped)
Salt (to taste)

<u>Toppings</u>
1 cup of sour cream
½ cup of scallions (chopped)
1 avocado- sliced
(Any toppings you like)

Preheat oven to 350 degrees.

For Sauce: In a saucepan over medium heat add (½ of the amount of vegetable oil), add onions and sauté until translucent. Add chili powder and stir in chicken stock, tomato puree and bring to a boil. Reduce to low heat and simmer 20 minutes. Season with salt to taste.

In another skillet pan over medium heat, add the rest of the vegetable oil, heat for 2 minutes. Then place the chicken cutlets in the skillet and cook 5 minutes on each side. Remove the chicken and when cooled—shred. In a bowl put the shredded chicken and add the cheese. With a generous spoonful of chicken/cheese, fill each flour tortilla and place each filled tortilla seam side down on a baking dish. Pour the sauce over the rolled chicken filled tortillas in the dish. Place in oven and bake for 30 minutes. Remove from the oven. Set aside for 5 minutes before topping with sour cream and scallions.

Serve hot.

Beef Tacos

1 pound of ground beef

2 tablespoons of chili powder

1 can of tomato paste

1-teaspoon garlic powder

2 tablespoons of cayenne pepper or hot sauce (to taste)

1 cup of water

2 tablespoons of vegetable oil

1 teaspoon of salt

1 teaspoon of pepper

8-10 corn tortillas (hard shell)

Toppings

1 cup of iceberg lettuce (shredded)

1 cup of monetary jack cheese (grated)

½ cup of red salsa (store bought)

½ cup of sour cream

1 avocado—sliced

In a medium skillet pan over medium heat add vegetable oil, heat for 2 minutes. Then add ground beef and cook for 15 minutes. Remove the beef from the pan and drain the fat of the beef into a strainer. Place the beef back into the same skillet over medium heat. Add chili powder, garlic powder, water and tomato paste. Stir to combine. Let simmer over low heat for 15 minutes.

To heat the tortillas shells, place in the oven for 5 minutes at 200 degrees. Once removing the tortilla shells from the oven, fill tortilla shells with beef mixture, then sprinkle cheese, avocado, lettuce and top with sour cream and salsa.

Serve hot.

Grilled Cheese
with a Kick

½ pound of monetary jack cheese (sliced)

2 tablespoons of butter (salted)

2 jalapeno peppers (diced)

8 slices of crusty bread (your choice)

    In large skillet pan over low-medium heat add butter (do not burn the butter). Place 4 slices of the bread into the pan. Top the bread with cheese, add jalapeno peppers and another layer of cheese and top with another piece of bread, cook for 3-5 minutes. Flip the sandwich and cook the other side for 3-5 minutes. Press down on the sandwiches—toasty sandwiches to serve.

    Serve hot.

Grilled Steak Fajitas

1 pound of trimmed skirt steak

2 tablespoons of vegetable oil

1 lime

2 garlic cloves

½ cup of jalapeno (sliced)

¼ cup of cilantro leaves (chopped)

Ten 7-inch flour tortillas (warmed)

Salt and pepper (to taste)

Toppings

Salsa (store bought)

½ cup of sour cream

½ cup of sliced red onions

Preheat charcoal grill or stovetop grill pan.

Rub the steak with oil, garlic, lime and jalapenos to marinate. Set aside for 30 minutes. Add the marinated steak into the grill pan. Grill the steak for 5-10 minutes on each side or until how you like the meat to be cooked (medium-rare). Transfer the steak to a cutting board surface and allow the steak to rest for a few minutes. Cut steak across the grain into thin slices.

In the same grill pan over medium heat add the peppers, onions and cilantro leaves and cook for 15 minutes, add salt and pepper to taste. Serve the steak with the peppers and onions immediately with tortillas and add toppings.

Serve hot.

Chapter Seven

Main Entrée

In-Between Man

A Compliment To The Meal

I'm finally all grown up! So why am I so insecure?

Before Shiny Penny, Rockefeller or Poppy, years ago, there were other men I met when I was in college that I had an interest in. Of course those interests weren't always fulfilled by an actual date. Sometimes just a brief moment of attraction with a friendly hello or a phone number exchange here or there. We have all met people who come in and out of our lives, but I met one man who surprisingly showed up every time I needed him or thought I did.

College was the first time he and I crossed paths. It was a path which crossed and carried over repeatedly for several years of my life, seemingly by chance. Our timing was on its own rhythm. We never kept in constant communication with each other. We would go months, even years, without seeing or speaking with each other. When we did see one another, he made me feel good about myself, healing my wounds from my broken relationships. It didn't matter how much time went by; we would just pick up where we left off. He was my In-Between Man.

Let me bring you back to the first time we met.

That memorable night was my 21st birthday and I was finally legal and a senior in college. I threw away my fake I.D. and went to a nightclub to dance like a rock star. My date had two left feet and needed to take a break. I, on the other hand was ripping up the floor.

That was when In-Between Man ever so smoothly danced his way over to me without spilling his drink. It was obvious he was no schoolboy. He was a mature, good-looking, stylish man and he was watching my every move. Knowing I wasn't single that night, he was flirty fishing with me.

As he hustled his way over on the dance floor towards me, we locked eyes and he unexpectedly said, "I've seen you before." He spoke of seeing me months earlier at a contest event. Finding out that the lady who he was on a date with at that contest event had won the New Hampshire local body-dance talent competition made me self-conscious. Not only was his date a knock out, she placed first prize!

Immediately, though I was flattered, I was uncomfortable accepting the compliment. I had just finally lost a great deal of weight during college, but it was hard for me to except being thinner and not still seeing myself as the chubby girl, ok, the fat girl!

On the dance floor I began to pull away as he twirled me and slipped me his business card. I was speechless. All I wanted to do was run back to my roommates like the school girl I was.

Three months later I called him. What can I say? He had been on my mind but I didn't want to call him from my dorm room. After I graduated I moved to Boston, got a job as the Manager of a hotel restaurant and I felt mature, more self-confident. Banking on my new found independence, I hoped it would come through and make me less insecure about having a date with the man who obviously dates prize winners.

He was able to take his eyes off a blue ribbon winner once; now it was time for me to accept that I too could be a winner. Whether he was my prize or not I wanted to find out and I was the only person standing in my way. Remember, he had given me his card, so it was up to me to make the second move.

It appeared as though In-Between Man was waiting for my call. Without hesitation, he made a dinner date with me. As I got ready for our date, feelings of excitement turned into a serious case of the nerves. Just getting comfortable in my own skin was hard enough, but I wasn't sure if In-Between Man knew that although outwardly I appeared mature, I was still only 21 years old at the time with a great deal of growing up to do.

He picked me up at my door, had a rose for me and made a reservation for a private room in the restaurant. It was just the two of us. As we got to know each other, it was obvious he had no idea that I was much younger than he thought and I had no idea he was fifteen years older than me! After the shock wore off, we both seemed to forget about the years on our birth certificates and enjoyed ourselves.

Dinner was like our first dance, filled with compliments. He could build up anyone's self-esteem and it felt great. It felt so great that we continued to date. After a two month whirlwind full of fun and excitement and of course him flattering me, I realized something was missing. "Houston we have a problem." We had not yet slept together—not even a nap. What was going on?

I finally asked him one night over dinner why we were not taking our relationship to the next level. Of course, if you ask that question, be ready to hear the answer. Unknown to me, he needed to make a decision. It seemed that there was a third party and he hadn't wanted to disrespect me by sleeping with me when he was already sleeping with her. Yes, "her", the blue ribbon winner was still on the runway! What? Come on! I can't compete with her! All my insecurities came barreling back. I made the decision for him. Bye-bye.

Six months had past and I was having lunch with some of my friends from Boston. Apparently In-Between Man had moved and was now a Boston city boy.

Our second attempt to date began shortly after. I asked him this time around if he was taken by another. He was all mine and very open to a relationship. He was so onboard that he introduced me to his mother at a dinner party at her house. We spent the night at his mother's beautiful home. It was full of love, tons of food and again separate bedrooms. I was ok with not sharing the covers with him at his mother's house. I completely respected the bedroom boundaries. Plus, I ate so much of her home cooking that I didn't think sexy came with bloating. That dinner let me see In-Between Man relaxed. He enjoyed his mother, family and of course her cooking; this busy man, who was an Executive came to a halt. He gave everyone a smile, a hug and laughter was exploding from everyone. This man was contagious!

When we left the next day, I was inspired to get to know him better. I mean bed better! Unfortunately, having a sleep over was not going to happen as soon as I wanted. In-Between Man had to take a business trip the very next day and would be traveling for a few weeks, so my love life was put on hold—and on hold and on hold! Are you kidding me? We still weren't having any bedtime stories after his three-week trip. We had several opportunities, but cupid was not on our side. Again, I said, bye-bye!

Four years later, I was living in New York City, after my break up Rockefeller, I kid you not; I got a voice message from In-Between Man. His business had moved to New Jersey, which was just a train ride away from me.

I decided to see him. I asked my girl friends for some advice. They all knew very well that In-Between Man and I had an on-off, sexless dating relationship for years. Their advice to me was, "Feel it out Denise. During dinner if you feel you're going to have a real relationship, do not sleep with him, but if it isn't going anywhere, go for it! You have nothing to lose."

In-Between Man and I made plans once again, but this time after I spoke with him my nerves were calm. I didn't feel that schoolgirl feeling anymore. We met at a romantic restaurant that he picked in the West Village. It was nice to see him, but I wasn't in awe of him anymore. I felt nothing. Not a damn thing. All his wonderful compliments over dinner didn't affect me as much as they had in the past. My schoolgirl crush was over. So I went for it—he was sleeping over!

As I walked him into my bedroom, I remembered what my girlfriends said, "I had nothing to lose." He was anxious about spending the night with me. I was closing that deal once and for all!

In the middle of our love session, my landline phone rang. The phone was in arm's length of me. I picked up the phone and hung it up without saying a word. Why would I pick up the phone, you ask? I couldn't take the chance of a flirty male friend or a girl friend leaving an obnoxious message. At that time my answering machine was an out loud message machine.

We continued our bedroom actives and the phone rang again. I could not believe this was happening! Again, I picked up the phone and hung it up. A few minutes went by and the phone rang for the third time. Now I was ticked off! I picked up the phone and threw it across the room. After all that time waiting to be with In-Between Man I was not going to let a ringing phone stop us.

The next night, I went out with the girls and let them know that there would be no future dates with In-Between

Man. "How was the sex?" they asked. "Not as good as the as dinner!"

There was no chemistry between us. After all that time the only tasty dish was on the restaurant's plate. I started to tell the girls about the phone ringing in the middle of our sex session. One of my wittiest friends said, "Did you hang up the phone before you threw it across the room?"

"What does that have to do with anything?" I replied.

"If you just threw the phone without hanging it up, how do you know that someone wasn't listening?" We all looked at each other with our eyes wide open wondered if indeed someone had heard my bedroom conversation!

Two days later I went out to lunch with a couple. They confessed that they were the ones calling me that night. Not only did they call but when I threw the phone across the room, my girl friend was right, the phone didn't disconnect. OMG!

After all that time, not only did I have sex with In-Between Man, but my friends did as well. No compliments there.

Food Talks!

Could it have been me who got in the way of a relationship? As a young woman I struggled with my weight, having low self-esteem. I craved the attention which In-Between-Man was offering me. He pumped me up in a way that was unique and frivolous. I was the one who couldn't get close. I only needed the compliments, not the man. Our conversations over every meal showed me the truth years later.

Tasty / Not Tasty—The Ingredients of In-Between Man:

<u>Tasty:</u> In a nightclub, over cocktails and dancing, In-Between Man danced his way right over to me. He never let anyone stop him, not even my date. I'm attracted to a man who is secure enough with himself to approach me no matter what.

<u>Tasty:</u> He wined and dined me. He made me feel so good about myself over every meal. I had never felt so special or pretty before I met him.

<u>Tasty:</u> At his mother's family dinner party, I saw a loving man who made everyone around him feel just as special. He was not a self-absorb man.

<u>Tasty:</u> When I was down and had the blues he was there for me, no questions asked. He was building my self-esteem every time we saw each other.

<u>Not Tasty:</u> Over every meal, I only ate up the compliments, I was addicted to them. My bad!

<u>Not Tasty:</u> Finding out over dinner that he had another woman on his plate wasn't what I'd ordered.

<u>Not Tasty:</u> I was the one that wouldn't let him get close. I was the one who wasn't giving off a sexual vibe every time we dated. I wasn't ready for him. I was too young to date a man fifteen years my senior.

<u>Not Tasty:</u> Years later, when I was more confident with who I was, his compliments were just compliments. I had grown out of the sweet nothings.

<u>Not Tasty:</u> At our last dinner together I made the choice to fulfill a sexually curiosity, which is never a good idea when your gut is telling you that there's no chemistry.

<u>Not Tasty:</u> Having a man on stand-by between relationships is not a healthy balanced meal for me.

A compliment can go a long way. In the case of In-Between Man, I let it go way too long!

Roast Beef & Red Skin Potatoes

2 pounds of center-cut beef tenderloin roast
½ cup of olive oil
1 tablespoon of butter
Optional: dijon or whole-grain mustard
4 red skin potatoes (wedged)
1 large clove of garlic (sliced)
Salt and pepper (to taste)

Preheat the oven to 400 degrees.

Heat a large ovenproof skillet over medium-high heat. Rub the beef with olive oil and season the beef all over with salt and a generous amount of pepper. Add the oil and butter in the skillet and heat, 2 minutes. Add the beef and sear until brown on all sides, about 10 minutes total.

Place the potatoes in a bowl add salt, pepper, garlic and olive oil. Place the potatoes in the skillet and place around the beef. Transfer the skillet to the oven.

Roast until an instant-read thermometer inserted in the center registers 125 degrees. For medium-rare, cook 40 minutes. Transfer the roast to a cutting board, tent very loosely with aluminum foil, let the roast rest for 5 minutes before slicing.

Serve hot.

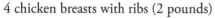

Mom's Chicken Stew

4 chicken breasts with ribs (2 pounds)
10 stalks of celery (diced)
10 carrots, peeled, and diced
½ cup of olive oil
1 large onion, chopped
1 can crushed tomatoes
1 can chicken broth
½ cup of fresh basil leaves, torn into pieces
1 can of tomato paste
3 large clove of garlic (diced)
½ teaspoon dried thyme leaves
1 can of beans (kidney or white beans (drained)
Grated Parmesan cheese (to taste)
Salt and pepper (to taste)

Heat the oil in a deep saucepan over medium heat. Add the celery, carrots and onions. Sauté the vegetables until the onions are golden, about 10 minutes. Add the chicken breasts and sauté until the chicken has a golden color. Add in the can of tomatoes, chicken broth, basil, tomato paste and thyme. Reduce to low heat and simmer, 45 minutes. Add the beans to the pot and continue to simmer, 20 minutes.

Take the chicken out of the saucepan and discard the skin and bones from the chicken breasts. Shred or cut the chicken into bite-size pieces. Return the chicken back to the saucepan. Add salt and pepper to taste. Pour the stew into soup bowls and top with grated Parmesan cheese.

Serve hot.

Marinated Flank Steak with Mushrooms

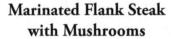

2 pounds of flank steak, trimmed

3 tablespoons of extra-virgin olive oil

2 tablespoons of red wine vinegar

½ cup of red wine

1 large clove garlic (sliced)

1 teaspoon of dijon mustard

1 package of button mushrooms, sliced (clean in warm water)

Salt and pepper (to taste)

To marinate the steak: Poke the steak all over with a fork. Place the steak in a large bowl. Add the olive oil, wine vinegar, red wine, garlic and the mustard. Season the steak with salt and pepper. Turn the steaks over and coat evenly. Cover and marinate the steaks at room temperature for 30 minutes.

Heat a large grill pan over medium-high heat or an outdoor grill. Remove the steak from the marinade. Cook the steaks for 10 minutes on each side for medium-rare. Set aside on a cutting board for 5 minutes. Cut the steak against the grain on an angle into thin slices. Place sliced mushrooms in the same grill pan, add salt and pepper with a splash of red wine. Sauté the mushrooms for 10 minutes over medium heat. Pour mushrooms over the steak.

Serve hot.

In-Between Man's Mother's Recipes
 Fried Lemon Flounder
with Butter and Capers

4 skinless flounder-fillets
½ cup of flour (for dredging fillets)
½ cup of vegetable oil
2 teaspoons of butter
2 lemons
½ cup of small capers
1 teaspoon of both salt and pepper

Clean fillets in cold water. Place fillets in a bowl, add cold water and squeeze lemon juice on the fillets. Set aside for 5 minutes. Remove the fillets and pat dry with paper towels. Pour flour onto a dish, add salt and pepper, and dredge fillets in flour.

Place oil and 1 teaspoons of butter in a flat skillet pan over medium-high until butter melts. Cook fish on each side, 5 minutes (cook more or less, depending on size of fillets) until the fillets turns a golden brown color and are crispy. Remove fish from the skillet to a serving dish.

In the same skillet over low-heat add in the remaining teaspoon of butter. Squeeze the remaining lemon and add the capers. Sauté together and pour the butter caper light sauce over fish fillets. Add salt and pepper to taste.

Sever hot.

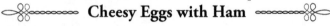

Cheesy Eggs with Ham

6 large eggs
¼ cup of water
1 cup of ricotta (whole milk)
½ cup minced scallion greens
1 tablespoon unsalted butter
¼ pound of ham (sliced)
Salt and black pepper (to taste)

    With a fork whisk the eggs and water. Melt butter in a small non-stick skillet over low-medium heat. Pour eggs into the skillet and let the eggs cook for about 3-5 minutes and gently stir with a rubber spatula until fluffy. Add the ricotta, chives and salt and pepper and evenly spread on top of the eggs. Continue cooking, stirring occasionally, until the eggs set into a soft creamy curd (if the eggs cook too long the cheese will begin to weep). Divide the eggs between 3-4 plates. In the same skillet add the ham and grill for 3 minutes on each side. Place the ham on the plate with the eggs and serve.

    Serve hot.

Chapter Eight

Main Entrée

The Professor

Learning How to Cook
Outside the Kitchen

"No thank you."

What else could I say to everyone who was trying to set me up on a blind date? My ego was in my way and it wouldn't let anyone play matchmaker. So what, I'm 30 years old and still single? Every woman is single again at some point in her lifetime. I just happen to be single again *several* times in my life!

I had no love interest, no prospects and since I really wasn't socializing as much as a single girl should I was able to save up a few dollars, as well as ask for a small family loan to open up my own company. Now, I was busy and broke! I created an interactive telecommunications company that was keeping me focused on business only, I had put my acting career on the shelf and all my girl friends were in relationships and I was dating my work. Trying to accomplish being a businesswoman in the corporate world was a great feeling. Not having a man to cuddle up with at night wasn't so great.

It was time for a change and there was only one thing I could do. I asked myself out on a date and I kept on asking. I was the best date a single girl could have. I took myself to the movies, dinners and shopping. I even gave myself a hug at the end of the night—that part was pathetic! I was just trying to nurture myself back into having a love life. I was ready to run in the dating marathon again.

It was a summer night and a guy friend of mine asked me to join him and his girlfriend for dinner. At the end of our meal, the frisky couple was going home to have a party for two. Being the third wheel, I went off to a restaurant's anniversary party I heard was happening in my neighborhood.

The party was packed and I couldn't find anyone who looked familiar, so I found a barstool, ordered myself a drink and became an easy target. After a few sips of my cocktail, I was surrounded. Not one man interested me and each pick up line became worse than the next. I could hear the bullshit getting thicker. It got so thick that all noise faded into the background as my eyes started to wander around the room. Finally when I was able to focus, I had locked eyes with The Professor.

"I know him. How do I know him?" Then it hit me. Six years prior, I had met this man at his club downtown in the

Meat Packing District. We were introduced to each other to work on a film project, which never got off the ground.

As I kept looking at him I could see he was aware that I was getting eaten alive by the male bar crowd. I knew this because the bouncer came over to me, moved some people out of the way and then head nodded to The Professor, letting him know I was fine. Though The Professor and I never spoke that night; it was just nice to know someone was watching out for me in a crowded restaurant.

Three weeks later, my girlfriend Annie and I went back to that same neighborhood restaurant for dinner. To my surprise, there was The Professor sitting at the bar talking to everyone. It turned out, he wasn't just a guest the night of the restaurant's anniversary party; he was the owner. A nice 40-year old Jewish boy from Queens, New York, who was built like a professional sports player, with a blue-eyed smile.

"We know each other" were the first words I said to him. I of course was hoping he remembered me from six years past, but he needed to be reminded. A quick casting story of how we met was all that was needed to spark his memory. I thanked him for being a gentleman and having his bouncer check on me the night of the party. That he remembered.

"Can I have your number Denise? We'll hang out and get a bite to eat next Thursday night." I wasn't sure if he was asking me out to be polite and wanted a new female friend in his life or was he asking me out on a date. "Hang out" aren't the words that make a girl feel a romantic vibe. "Sure, just call me on Wednesday, we'll go from there."

Wednesday came and he never called, "Seriously!"

Thursday he did. He was confirming what time we were getting together later that night for dinner at his restaurant. His confidence was apparent and his need for me to pick up a lint brush before I met him was over confident. Did he really just ask me to go to the store before meeting him at the restaurant and pick up a lint brush? He definitely is asking me out as a friend only!

Shocked by his request, I actually contemplated going to the store. I was also shocked when I met him at his restaurant and I wasn't the only person he asked out. The Professor had invited a good friend of his, David, as well. There the three of us were having some appetizers and drinks and I now had to get to know two men in one night. The evening was interesting and getting to know The Professor was challenging. Everyone wanted his attention. Having his friend David there worked out for me. I didn't want to sit there alone most of the night. Nice guys, but too much work for one girl, me! I was looking to date just one man. No thank you, goodnight.

Hours later that same night, The Professor called me and wanted to see me again. The late hour was not on his mind, asking me out to dinner again was. "I'd love too" was all I needed to say. From that point on The Professor called me every day, not bringing up when we were having dinner together again, just a hello to touch base with me. "What happened to our dinner date?" was all I was thinking about.

Even though I was attracted to him I told him to stop calling me. If he couldn't make a date, then I couldn't make the time. "What's with this guy?" I wasn't looking for a new guy friend. There would be no chance for romance if I only thought of him as a guy friend who kept calling me to just say hello. Good-bye!

A few days later, after I took away his phone privileges, The Professor finally stepped it up a notch and told me where we would be having our dinner date—at his restaurant. Is he cheap or location-ally challenged? Okay, I gave him a break and didn't mention we've been there before or should I say that was the only place we've been. At least we'll be sitting at a table and sharing a meal alone. He took his first step in the right direction. It's a date!

The marathon had begun. We were out every night. We were Rock Stars! The Professor was the King of New York. Everybody, and I mean everybody, knew him.

The Professor was so well known that we were invited to every event, every dinner party, every opening of a restaurant/nightclub. I loved the rush, but oh my God, I was exhausted! We had only dated a month and I didn't know if I was coming or going. What I did know was my name way too well. "Denise, Denise, Denise" was all I heard from him over countless dinners. This guy was killing me.

As self-efficient as The Professor was, he would ask me to assist him with everything he was doing or wanted. "Denise can you get me my phone, my date book and yes, we'll do my laundry when we're done eating. "We'll?" He meant me!

Doing his laundry and cleaning up our takeout; I needed to sit down, so I came up with a plan. I thought if I started cooking for him my hands would be too busy to do anything for him and his mouth would be too busy chewing to request anything more from me. Wrong! Denise, Denise, Denise!

My cooking reminded him of his mother's food. When I met his mother I could only fall in love with her. Mother Molly, a warm, loving, traditional, strong, mother who put her love into her food.

I learned that one of The Professor's favorite dishes was his mother's "Spinach Latkes." I got a "hands on" cooking lesson the first time I met Mother Molly at their family home. She taught me how to replicate that traditional family recipe. The entire family would arm wrestle for the last spinach latke. The Professor had no worries about losing the match since I just learned how to keep alive the traditional flavor of his mother's dish.

Going to Mother's Molly's for dinner every few weeks was something I looked forward to. The Professor always wanted to know what she was serving for diner before we arrived to her home; not afraid to ask her for what he wanted on his plate, as she was not afraid to hang the phone up on him in mid-sentence. "Mom, mom, mom?"

Truthfully I never knew if Mother Molly's hang-ups were concluding the conversation or she was just over him. I should have bought Molly a sign to hang in her kitchen that said, "No Requests!"

Both his mother and I had the same flair for Mediterranean cooking so it was easy for me to make The Professor feel like he was in his childhood home every time I surprised him with a meal. The surprise for me was he still thought his mother was there to serve him hand and foot, clear the table and wipe his face. I'm surprised he didn't ask me to burp him.

When I wasn't catering to The Professor we were out on the town eating and drinking. Still he depended on me to read the menu to him. When I read off a dish that lit up his eyes, there was no going back to what maybe I wanted. Giving in to him was easier but that resulted in me ordering late night takeout to satisfy my taste buds and yes, his mouth always wanted a taste. There was no appetite suppressant for The Professor.

When it came to his sexual appetite he was able to order for himself and I was the only entrée on the menu. He had his PHD in the bedroom and after studying "under" him, I made the Dean's list. Hence is nickname, The Professor. Though our intimacy was great, his need for me to do errands and tasks for him was greater and endless. Our relationship became more of a friendship and three months later we broke up.

We continued to talk during the break up and eventually we reunited. The Professor was used to his past girlfriends or as I like to call them, "bubble gum girls" who always waited on him hand and foot. He wore me down and I became this "I'll do it all type girlfriend." Needy or not, we were embracing every minute together and got along incredibly. Restaurants, coffee shops, café's – always great food and always together; we were so attached that on his birthday he must of thought it was my birthday as well – he bought me roses!

At his birthday party we invited over 600 people to a nightclub for an endless buffet and to dance the night away. We were always laughing; we were best friends but our love life took a major back seat.

The fear of breaking up again and losing our friendship was apparent to both of us. We kept on going and hung in there but the pressure of not having enough bedroom time was weighing heavily on our relationship and a home cooked meal became our substitute spice instead of the bedroom.

After three years of an intense relationship—not even a great meal together could not stop the inevitable. We were over, finished, done.

A few months later The Professor called me. I was surprised but curious so I took the call. It was just a friendly "hello." No "I miss you Denise." It upset me a bit, so I went for his gut — literally!

"Got to go, I have company coming over and I'm making "Spinach Latkes."

"What?" He replied. "You're making my mother's spinach latkes!" I had to pull the phone away from my ear. The power of a man's mother's food is like no other. Needless to say, I was the one now left holding the phone, "Hello, hello, hello?"

Food Talks!

In the case of The Professor, my food experiences with him told me from the first time he asked me out, to sitting at home and sharing a meal with him, he wasn't looking for a girlfriend; he was looking for a stepmother.

Tasty/Not Tasty: The Ingredients of The Professor:

<u>Tasty:</u> Though The Professor and I never spoke that night of the restaurant's anniversary party, it was nice to

know someone was watching out for me. A man that can keep an eye on the food, cocktails and his staff serving his patrons was impressive. But the "Special" for the evening was keeping an eye on me!

Not Tasty: He asked me to "hang out." That's how he asked me out on our first date. Then he called on the day of the date. He was confirming what time we were getting together *later* that night. Ladies, I need a man to call the night before and asking me to "hang out?" well that's just not sexy.

Not Tasty: As he was making plans to have me meet him at his restaurant, The Professor asked me to pick up a lint brush. Right then and there the food experience of what he was saying the first time he asked me out to his restaurant on a date was telling me so much about this man. His request was telling me he was already having me serve him.

Not Tasty: He had invited his good friend David out on our first date. Cocktails for three! Really ladies, do I need to say anymore? No.

Tasty: Hours later after our first date The Professor called me and asked me out to a real dinner date. Anytime a man I like asks me out, it is always a compliment, even in the wee hours—didn't bother me.

Not Tasty: Our dinner date was planned. But he picked his restaurant again! He was playing it too safe for me or was it that he knew he would be waited on hand and foot because he was the owner. He liked to be waited on—that was a fact!

Not Tasty: "Denise, Denise, Denise" was all I heard. I'd like to sit down and eat my food too. The Professor never ceased wanting, regardless of what I was doing.

<u>Tasty:</u> My recipes reminded him of his mother's cooking and he loved his mother. A man who loves his mother is needed for my Recipe for Love.

Not Tasty: Even during a meal. He thought his girlfriend, me, was always going to serve him. I too would like to ring a bell and say, "Garcon!"

Not Tasty: When I read off a dish from a menu that lit up his eyes, there was a turning back to what maybe I wanted to eat. Hello, I'm here too!

<u>Tasty:</u> At his birthday party, with all the great food and cocktails and people giving him so much attention—The Professor had me by his side the entire night and never asked me for anything. We should have had his birthday party once a month!

When it came to my plate of life, it was too full of The Professor and for me that was too large of an order to swallow. Today, Mother Molly's "Spinach Latkes" are still one of my favorite dishes to make.

Stuffed Grape Leaves

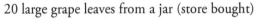

20 large grape leaves from a jar (store bought)

1 pound of ground lamb (beef or turkey)

¼ cup of vegetable oil

1 cup of onion finely chopped

2 garlic cloves, finely chopped

½ cup long-grain rice

3 tablespoons toasted pine nuts

½ cup chopped fresh mint

2 cups chicken stock

½ cup fresh lemon juice

Salt and pepper (to taste)

Remove grape leaves from the jar and rinse each of the grape leaves well. Snip off the stems. Set aside. Pat dry with paper towel and stack on top of each other. In a skillet pan, heat 2 tablespoons of the vegetable oil and add the onion until soft. Add garlic and cook for 5 minutes. Add the meat and rice, stirring to combine.

Stir in pine nuts, mint, salt, pepper and ½ cup of the chicken stock. Bring to a simmer and cook until all of the liquid is evaporated, stirring occasionally. Remove the skillet from the heat.

Allow the meat and rice mixture to cool completely. Place a grape leaf smooth side down with the stem end toward you. Place a tablespoon of the cooled meat and rice filling near the stem end, fold in the sides of the leaf over the filling. Beginning with the stem end and roll up the leaf, not too tightly because the rice will grow. Continue and repeat process for remaining grape leaves. Transfer the stuffed grape leaves to a deep saucepot, just large enough to contain all stuffed grape leaves layering on top on each other.

Add 2 cups chicken stock with the lemon juice over the stuffed grape leaves, add water if necessary to just barely cover stuffed grape leaves. Place a dish on top of the rolled filled grape leaves (so they don't unwrap). Cover the pot and over low-medium heat, bring the liquid to a simmer and cook until tender, about 45 minutes. Remove the pot from heat, uncover and allow cooling.

Serve warm or room temperature.

Yogurt Chicken
with Herbs

4-6 skinless chicken cutlet halves

2 tablespoons vegetable oil

1 lime

3 tablespoons chicken broth, homemade or low-sodium, canned

1 cup of yogurt (Greek)

2 cloves of garlic (smashed)

2 tablespoons packed fresh mint leaves (chopped)

Salt and black pepper (to taste)

Clean the chicken in cold water thoroughly. Place the chicken in a bowl. Add salt, pepper, lime, yogurt, garlic and mint. Set aside for 1 hour or refrigerate overnight.

Heat the oil in a medium size skillet over medium-high heat. Place chicken cutlets in the skillet. Cook the chicken on each side for about 5-7 minutes. Transfer the chicken cutlets to a plate.

Add the remaining yogurt sauce to the skillet and let simmer on low heat for 10 minutes. Pour the yogurt sauce over the chicken cutlets.

Serve hot.

Couscous with
Toasted Almonds and Raisins

1 ½ cups couscous
2 tablespoons butter (salted)
1 cup of blanched almonds (sliced)
1 cup of raisins
1-teaspoon ground cumin
¼ teaspoon ground turmeric
½ teaspoon ground coriander
½ teaspoon sweet paprika
1-teaspoon sea salt
3 cups vegetable stock
Salt and pepper (to taste)

To prepare the almonds and raisins mixture. Heat the butter in a sauté pan over low-medium heat until it is melted. Add the almonds, raisins, cumin, turmeric, coriander, paprika and salt. Stir until the almonds start to brown about 5 minutes. Let cool.

To prepare the couscous. Heat the vegetable stock in a saucepan over medium-high heat and add season with salt and pepper. Place the couscous in a large bowl, pour the hot stock over the couscous and cover with a plate or foil. Let stand until the stock is absorbed, about 10 minutes. When the couscous has absorbed the stock, fluff with a fork. Add the almonds and raisin mixture and mix well. Season to with salt and pepper to taste

Serve warm.

Stuff Peppers

1 pound of ground (lamb, chicken or beef)

6 red, green or yellow bell peppers

1 cup white rice (uncooked)

3 tablespoons of vegetable oil

2 cloves of garlic

1 pound of ground (lamb, chicken or beef)

1 teaspoon dried basil

½ cup fresh chopped parsley

2 cups chicken stock

2 scallions, chopped

1 can of tomatoes

2 lemons

Preheat oven to 350 degrees F.

Place rice in a bowl of cold water and let sit for 15 minutes. In a saucepan over low- medium heat add the can of tomatoes and squeeze in the juice of the lemon. Simmer for 20 minutes. Remove from heat.

In a medium skillet pan over medium heat add oil, garlic, parsley and scallions and sauté for 5 minutes. Add the meat and cook about 10 minutes.

Drain the water from the rice and pour the rice into the skillet and mix well with the meat. Then remove from the stovetop.

Slice off the tops of bell peppers. Remove seeds and discard and wash the peppers. Stuff the peppers with the meat and rice mixture. Place the stuffed peppers in a square-baking dish. Pour the tomato lemon sauce over the stuffed peppers. Place in oven and bake at 350 degrees for 45 minutes or until tender.

Serve hot.

The Professor's Mother's Recipes

The Famous
Spinach Latkes

1 package of frozen spinach (thawed out—microwave for 5 minutes)
6 eggs (or 3 eggs and 3 egg whites)
½ cup of grated Parmesan cheese
2 tablespoons of breadcrumbs (seasoned)
1 small onion finely chopped
1 teaspoon of salt and pepper

In a medium bowl, add spinach, eggs, Parmesan cheese, breadcrumbs, onions, salt and pepper. Mix well with a fork. The mixture should be light and soupy. In a medium skillet pan over low-medium heat, add oil. Simmer until hot, about 2 minutes. Once oil is hot, take a teaspoon and spoon out the spinach egg mixture into the skillet. Making little round circles (little pancakes). Cook for about 3-5 minutes on each side. Repeat the process until all the spinach mixture is finished. Once cooked, place the spinach latkes on paper towels and lightly pat, absorbing the oil.

Serve room temperature.

Chapter Nine

Side Dishes

"Side Dishes!"

"It was really nice meeting you. Would you like to get together sometime?"

It's Ladies Night once again! Ladies get in the shower, put on your make-up, get dressed and let's go find ourselves a man!

The Dating Scene:

I mentally had to prepare myself for the elimination process. Some people enjoy the dating scene—I don't know any of those people, but I hear that they do exist. Most people date for the obvious, to find their next special someone, which is not an easy task. It takes a great deal of effort, but it must be done. You have to get out of your home and do the work—socialize!

What's the worst that can happen? For me, it was when I would meet a man at a social place (a venue of food) and he would do everything to get my attention. We'd have a long conversation together, have a drink and maybe bite to eat together and just as I would be leaving he'd ask me ever so politely for my phone number, **only not to use it!** My food experience has spoken: "He is not for you Denise!"

I've had my share of "Side Dishes" good and not so good. The one's I share with you in my story, I wouldn't re-order them again; however, I wouldn't change any of those dating experiences because they ALL added up to me learning that Food Talks. Even a first dining date can speak the loudest.

I've added my own personal side dish recipes to describe them.

Side Dish
Hot & Cold

I was working on a project and would frequently dine at this corner restaurant in Midtown Manhattan. The bartender there was concentrating more on me than what he was pouring in his drinks. After several attempts of him trying to get me to go on a dinner date, I gave in. It wasn't that I wasn't physically attracted to him; I just don't shit where I eat!

This handsome bartender was always attentive to me and I do like a man who's persistent. He wasn't taking my excuse, "I'm busy" as a no thank you. So, I said yes. How bad could the date be?

On the evening of the date, he called me the hour he was to pick me up, telling me he was going to be an hour late. I should have cancelled but I was already dressed, starving and I wanted to be able to show my face again at his place of work. I sucked it up! "Okay", was all I could say.

When he showed up that rainy night, he was soaking wet, had no umbrella and didn't even plan where we were eating. Are you kidding me? I had to take charge. I grabbed my umbrella, hailed us a cab, picked the restaurant; I mean someone had to be the man on this date!

Over dinner, when he said, "I'm not sure I have my I.D on me?" Those were the last words my legal self wanted to hear from him. He could serve liquor, I just wasn't sure he could drink it. "Please don't ask for his I.D" was all I was thinking when the waiter approached our table.

We order dinner, and all hell broke loose!

He hated everything! He hated work, his family, his apartment, his last relationship and he even hated ice cream. Who hates ice cream? I was listening in disbelief that he had all this anger and he was overwhelming me on our first date. I felt sorry for him, until he let me see what else he hated.

The bus-boy approached our table to clear the dishes and my date told him that I wasn't finished. I said, "Thank you, but I am finished." Again, he turned to the bus-boy, "She's not!" Back and forth we went.

"Do you want to eat the rest of my dinner?"

He leaned forward in response to me, "When I buy you dinner Denise, you eat all of it. That cost me $22.00!" He then leaned back and lit up a cigarette. I too leaned back, watched him light his cigarette, asked him for a drag and I never took my eyes off of him. With a mission, I inhaled the smoke, blew it in his face and put the cigarette out in my food! "Do you think I'm finished now?"

I miss that Midtown restaurant.

Not Tasty: Everything!

Roasted Potatoes with Homemade Ketchup

Roasted Potatoes

4-5 medium russet potatoes (sliced)

3 cloves garlic, sliced

¼ cup extra-virgin olive oil

¼ cup of hot sauce

1 lemon

Salt and pepper (to taste)

Homemade Ketchup

3 pounds ripe tomatoes

2 tablespoons extra-virgin olive oil

1 medium onion (finely diced)

2 cloves garlic, minced

¼ cup cider vinegar

Salt and pepper (to taste)

Preheat the oven to 400 degrees.

Roasted Potatoes:

Scrub the potatoes with warm water well. I prefer to keep the skins on. Slice the potatoes and place potatoes in a bowl. Add garlic, extra virgin olive oil, squeeze the juice from the lemon, hot sauce and salt and pepper. Mix well and pour out potatoes on to a baking sheet pan. Place potatoes in the oven for 30-40 minutes until crispy.

Serve hot.

Homemade Ketchup:

In a small saucepan heat 2 tablespoons of olive oil over medium heat. Add the onions, until the onions are golden brown, about 10 minutes. Add the garlic, vinegar and brown sugar. Stir until slightly thickening.

Core and chop the tomatoes with their skins on. Add the chopped tomatoes to the saucepan. Reduce to low heat, stirring occasionally, until thickened, 15 minutes. Remove saucepan from heat and pour into a blender to puree. Pour the warm ketchup out of the blender and into a bowl and cover with plastic wrapping. Place in the refrigerator for at least 2 hours or overnight.

Serve both.

Side Dish
Adam & Eve

Not only did I bite the apple, I ate the whole entire core, seeds and all!

I was at a party when we were introduced. We'll call him "Adam." We had some light conversation and exchanged business cards. Harmless! We both were in relationships at the time and they too were at the party. I had no attraction to Adam, just business.

About 2 years later Adam and I finally made a plan to meet for a business lunch. We ordered steak, lobster, drinks and we had an immediate attraction. Business? What?

"How's your boyfriend Denise?"

"You mean my ex-boyfriend."

"How's your girlfriend?"

Over lunch he informed me his relationship had also ended. He had moved out of his ex's apartment and was now staying with a "female friend" until he could find a new place for himself.

"Female friend?" Is that code for this Irishman-Catholic man? Meaning, "girlfriend?"

What did it matter? I was there for business and I was just enjoying some playful attention from a handsome, smart, successful man who happened to be a huge flirt—until things changed. The next thing I knew our business lunch turned into an evening out on the town.

"Did he just kiss me?"

I went home that night thinking why did I kiss him back? My principals flew right out the window once I kissed him! He's living with a woman, I don't know him and is he telling me the truth—female friend?

That will never happen again, I told myself. It didn't happen again; well, not until I saw him the next night. Over a few dates we were drawn together like two magnets.

"Did you find a new apartment yet?"

"I'm still looking."

I just wanted him to move forward and find his new place, so I waited and waited. During the waiting period he would always make dinner plans for the upcoming week with me. Sometimes he would cancel dinner, too many times. Hmm? Then he would call me that very same night and say, "I can meet you for dinner now." Hmm?

Almost every place we dined, everyone knew him; the owners, the bartenders, but most of all, the ladies. I mean almost every woman knew him. Something was wrong so I started pushing him away. Standing my ground, the truth came at me like a lighten bolt!

"I'm getting married."

He did tell me the truth over our first lunch. He was living with his female friend.

Not Tasty: He just left out the part that she was his Fiancée.

Adam & Eve
Apple Crepes

<u>Crepes</u>
4 eggs
1 cup flour
1½-cups milk
½ cup of apple juice
2 tablespoons brown sugar
Powder sugar (to taste)

<u>Filling</u>
4 golden delicious apples
½ cup of raisins
1 tablespoon of honey
1 teaspoon of cinnamon
¼ cup apple juice

<u>Crepes:</u>
In a blender or food processor mix together, eggs, flour, milk, apple juice and sugar. Blend until smooth. In a non-stick crepe-pan over high heat, add 1-teaspoon butter or vegetable oil and heat for 2 minutes. Pour about 2 tablespoons batter into pan, spread batter evenly to cover entire surface. Cook until it browns around the edges, about 30 seconds. Flip the crepe over with a spatula and cook until it starts to brown, another 30 seconds. Slide the crepe onto a plate and continue the same process until all the batter is finished.

Filling:

Peel, core and dice apples. In a small saucepan over low-medium heat, add the apples, raisins, honey, cinnamon and apple juice cook until apples are soft but not mushy. Then spoon fill onto a crepe and fold twice. Powder sugar on top and serve.

Side Dish
Fashion Faux Pas

Girl's night!

I met my girl friend Annie for dinner and we sat at the bar waiting for our table. The man who was sitting next to me interrupted us and started a conversation. No pickup lines, just started talking, but "he" was the only one speaking. Annie and I were catching up with each other and this man just kept talking to us. We couldn't get a word in. He would not shut-it!

"Chatty Kathy" needed to be interrupted, "I'm Denise." When he introduced himself, he gave me his full name. Annie grabbed my attention to let me know "who he was." It turned out that his name was his label. He was a well-known Fashion Designer. I was clueless. He asked me for my number and kept asking as we were trying to taste our wine. I just gave it to him so he'd stop talking. I really wasn't interested.

I wasn't attracted to him and I don't date men because they are rich and famous. He was persistent and kept on calling me for weeks. I finally accepted his dinner invitation. To me, it was to be just a friendly dinner date. When he picked me up at my apartment he asked to come up for a drink. He wanted to have a few drinks before we went out, I didn't!

As soon as he walked through my door he began to babble and I noticed that his shirt was drenched with perspiration. He was speaking so fast, I handed him a glass of wine to mellow him out.

That night was the opening night of a New York City hotspot restaurant and my date was one of the invited "Celebrity Personalities." I was born in the day, but I wasn't born yesterday. He wasn't sober, and drinking wasn't why.

"Are you on something?"

"No, not at all! I used to take drugs but I haven't lately."

Lately?

I wanted him out of my apartment. The more I pulled away the more he begged me to give him a chance. He was an obnoxious sweaty man who would not stop talking or leave my home. I had no choice; the only way I was getting him out of my apartment was for me to leave with him.

He had his car parked in front of my building with his driver. As we were getting into the car, I told him he needed to change his soaking wet shirt. He must have been a pro at being a hot sweaty mess because his driver handed him a freshly ironed shirt from the trunk of the car.

Once we were at the party, he introduced me to his friends. I was polite and gracious to them. I wanted to have a nice drink so I ordered for myself and told him I was hungry and wanted to just sit down to eat. He walked me over to a table where there was a mountain of cheese and said, "Here you go, knock yourself out." He was lucky I didn't knock him out!

As a piece of cheese touched my mouth, he said, "Stay right here, I'll be right back." There I was at this party dipping myself in cheese fondue. I could not believe this was happening to me!

I looked around the restaurant to see if I know anyone. I saw a male friend of mine across the room; I walked over to him and told him my date left me at the cheese table to dine. While we were speaking, a woman over heard my date's name.

She turned to me and said, "I thought he was in rehab?"

Not Tasty. From the moment I met "Chatty Kathy" sitting at the bar, he had already inhaled his appetite suppressant, which wasn't on the recovery menu.

Macaroni & Cheese

1 pound elbow macaroni

2 pints of milk (whole or 2%)

½ stick of butter

1 tablespoon flour

1 tablespoon salt

2 tablespoons dry or wet mustard

2 cups American cheese

1 cup grated Monterey Jack cheese

1-½ cups shredded cheddar cheese (sharp)

1-½ cups grated Parmesan cheese

½ cup breadcrumbs (seasoned)

Preheat the oven to 400 degrees.

Boil 3 cups water in a medium size pot. Add a few drops of oil and salt and add macaroni. Stir and cook for 5 minutes (not fully cooked). Drain the macaroni, pour it back in the pot and set it aside.

In a medium size saucepan, heat milk over low heat and stir in butter and flour to thicken, 10 minutes. Add salt, mustard, and ¼ cup of water. Reduce heat to simmer. Gradually stir in all the cheeses with a wooden or metal spoon. Continue to cook, stirring constantly until the cheese has melted and the sauce is smooth, about 10 minutes. Pour elbow macaroni into the cheese sauce. Mix well and pour the entire mixture into a medium baking dish, top with breadcrumbs. Place bake dish into the oven and bake until bubbling and top browned, about 30 minutes. Set aside for 10 minutes.

Serve hot.

Chapter Ten

Recipe for Love Ingredient's Card

Recipe for Love Ingredient's Card:

Time to get your pen out!

You are going to make your own, "Recipe for Love Ingredient's Card."

Write down the10 Tasty ingredients you want in a man. Write down the 10 Not Tasty ingredients you don't want in a man.

We all know we don't get everything we want, that's life!

Prioritize what you must have on the Tasty list, then only chose 5 Tasty(s) and cross out what you can live without. Do the same for the Not Tasty list. Chose the top 5 that you DON"T want at all and put those on your Not Tasty list, and cross out what you could live with. Now you have your 10 ingredients which becomes your "Recipe for Love."

Let's make your "Recipe for Love Ingredient's Card."

Tasty:

1. _____
2. _____
3. _____
4. _____
5. _____
6. _____
7. _____
8. _____
9. _____
10. _____

Not Tasty:

1. _____
2. _____
3. _____
4. _____
5. _____
6. _____
7. _____
8. _____
9. _____
10. _____

Recipe for Love
Top Ten Ingredients

Tare this page out of the book and carry it in your purse

Tasty: (Wants)

1. _____
2. _____
3. _____
4. _____
5. _____

Not Tasty: (Don't Want—at ALL)

1. _____
2. _____
3. _____
4. _____
5. _____

Remember, the "Not Tasty" list is where the food speaks the loudest. If your food experiences with your date puts him on the "already trimmed down" Not Tasty list of what you don't want—Clear your plate of him and re-order!

Bon appétit!